How Communication Scholars Think and Act

2/10/17

To Lisa,

May we connect
about these ideas
and more for a
long time to come.

Warmly,

Julien

LIFESPAN
COMMUNICATION
Children, Families, and Aging

Thomas J. Socha
GENERAL EDITOR

Vol. 11

The Lifespan Communication series
is part of the Peter Lang Media and Communication list.
Every volume is peer reviewed and meets
the highest quality standards for content and production.

PETER LANG
New York • Bern • Frankfurt • Berlin
Brussels • Vienna • Oxford • Warsaw

Julien C. Mirivel

How Communication Scholars Think and Act

A Lifespan Perspective

PETER LANG
New York • Bern • Frankfurt • Berlin
Brussels • Vienna • Oxford • Warsaw

Library of Congress Cataloging-in-Publication Data

Names: Mirivel, Julien C., author.
Title: How communication scholars think and act: a lifespan perspective /
Julien C. Mirivel.
Description: New York: Peter Lang, 2017.
Series: Lifespan communication: children, families, and aging; Vol. 11
ISSN 2166-6466 (print) | ISSN 2166-6474 (online)
Includes bibliographical references and index.
Identifiers: LCCN 2016040467 | ISBN 9781433130793 (hardcover: alk. paper)
ISBN 978-1-4331-3078-6 (paperback: alk. paper)
ISBN 978-1-4539-1913-2 (ebook pdf)
ISBN 978-1-4331-3788-4 (epub) | ISBN 978-1-4331-3789-1 (mobi)
Subjects: LCSH: Communication—Study and teaching.
Classification: LCC P91.3 M57 2017 | DDC 302.2—dc23
LC record available at https://lccn.loc.gov/2016040467
DOI: 10.3726/978-1-4539-1913-2

Bibliographic information published by **Die Deutsche Nationalbibliothek**.
Die Deutsche Nationalbibliothek lists this publication in the "Deutsche
Nationalbibliografie"; detailed bibliographic data are available
on the Internet at http://dnb.d-nb.de/.

The paper in this book meets the guidelines for permanence and durability
of the Committee on Production Guidelines for Book Longevity
of the Council of Library Resources.

© 2017 Peter Lang Publishing, Inc., New York
29 Broadway, 18th floor, New York, NY 10006
www.peterlang.com

Printed in the United States of America

This book is dedicated to Bill
For inspiring me and showing me the way

CONTENTS

Acknowledgments   ix

Chapter 1. The Communication Professorate   1
Chapter 2. What Is the Nature of the Communication Professorate?   15
Chapter 3. How Do Communication Professors Grow?   37
Chapter 4. How Do Communication Professors View Teaching?   49
Chapter 5. How Do Communication Professors Think?   65
Chapter 6. What Do Communication Professors See and Hear?   77
Chapter 7. How Do Communication Professors
           Communicate Across their Career?   91
Chapter 8. What Behaviors Do Communication Professors Value?   109
Chapter 9. What Can We Learn From Communication Professors?   131

           Appendix A: Semi-Structured Interview Schedule   143
           Appendix B: Participants   147
           Index   149

ACKNOWLEDGMENTS

This book was made possible by the care, work, and dedication of many people. I'm grateful for Mary Savigar at Peter Lang who saw potential in an idea and encouraged me to transform it into a book project. I also am thankful to two of my graduate students at the University of Arkansas at Little Rock, Kristina Godfrey and Amanda Pasierb, who supported this project by conducting interviews, transcribing data, and more importantly for reflecting on these ideas with me.

I wrote this book while serving as Interim Chair in a department outside of my discipline. During that time, I was blessed to have Rocio Roles, a doctoral student in Criminal Justice, working with me as my research assistant. Rocio's positive energy, work ethic, attention to details, and support for this project was simply amazing: thank you Rocio.

I also have a great amount of gratitude for all of the communication professors who participated in the study. Spending time in conversation with all of them was a gift in itself. I hope to have done justice to the similarities that exist among them and our common desire to improve the way people communicate with one another. A special thanks goes to Carol Thompson, Michael Kleine, and Allan Ward; three colleagues I admire who got the interviews started.

I want to give a special thank you to my mother, Annick Vauthier, for providing her beautiful artwork for the cover of my first book and this one. Thank you, Maman, for giving life to the writing.

Writing a book is nice, but it is even better when you are surrounded by a loving family. My favorite conversations are always at home with my 2-year-old John Luke (or as I say it "Jean-Luc"), my 9-year-old Hugo, and my wonderful wife Meg, who believes in me always. Thank you for the laughs and the love, and for being in my life.

· 1 ·

THE COMMUNICATION
PROFESSORATE

On a dry fall day, I receive an e-mail from Lacie, a student at the university where I work. After greeting me, she writes: "I have to choose a minor to go with my psych degree and wanted to talk about some of the avenues with criminal justice that would coincide." She adds, "possibly profiling or would that be through the police department? I have no idea about that." In her last line before a nice "thanks," she writes: "Just whenever you have time! Everyone keeps trying to push me towards social work, but I know that's not for me." Then, she signs off with "Have a wonderful day." I love that, and I call Lacie immediately to set up a time to meet.

When we get together, she comes into my office, which is located on the 5th floor of a founding building on campus. We sit next to each other and I listen to see what she is after. In our conversation, she says she has not found her niche yet. She enjoys psychology, but she doesn't seem convinced by it. She explains that she is introspective and introverted. She says, "I pay attention to the people around me and I wish the world could be better" and "I think a lot about how to do the right thing and I want to help people. I am sensitive to what people feel and do, and observant; and I want to be ethical." As I am listening to Lacie, I can see bits and pieces of me and my colleagues in the Department of Speech Communication.

Lacie's introversion reminds me of Carol and Gerald, who are gentle, attentive, powerfully sensitive, and who also need to regain energy on their own. She enjoys writing, meeting with people, and as she cued in the last line of her e-mail, wants to inspire people to be positive and kind. Lacie, I am beginning to see, needs to be a Communication Major—she would be happy there and surrounded by people who experience the world in similar ways, as the project in this book taught me. And that is exactly what I told her.

Seven days after our meeting, I receive another note from Lacie. "Well," she wrote, "I am now a speech communication major." "It became increasingly clear," she adds, "where I belong." By claiming her major, Lacie made the first step on living the life of a communication professional. In the next several years, she will take courses in interpersonal communication, organizational communication, ethics, and, of course, public speaking. She will graduate with a bachelor's degree in communication and may continue on to earn a master's or even a doctorate degree. She may even become an assistant professor, earn tenure, make contributions to ways of thinking that we have yet to imagine, and impact the lives of countless students. She alone will choose that path, but wouldn't it be helpful if she could see what her professional life might be like? What challenges and blessings are part of it? And what makes it valuable, meaningful, and worth the effort? This book seeks to answer these questions and may help students such as Lacie to envision their future.

This is a book about the experiences of 30 accomplished scholars in the communication discipline. All of them are faculty members who have earned a PhD in the field of communication and have been teachers, scholars, and often administrators for at least 25 years after earning their doctorate. Together, the 30 faculty members who were interviewed have produced a tremendous amount of teaching, research, and service. All of them have taught many communication courses at all levels that cut across areas of study. Many have won distinguished awards in teaching, research, and service. Together, they have produced hundreds of books, thousands of journal articles and conferences presentations, and countless workshops. They have served as graduate coordinators, chairs of departments, deans of colleges, and presidents of professional associations. Eight have been presidents of the National Communication Association and two have been presidents of the International Communication Association. In short, these communication professors have been, and continue to be, incredibly productive. But this book is not about how to be productive, how to publish, or even how to teach better. It is about the natural development that unfolds for a person who is studying communication.

This book explores the journey of the "communication professorate," a term I use to describe individuals who have been active in the academic side of the communication discipline throughout their lifespan. They have engaged their mind and body in reflecting about, and enacting, communication. Not only have they studied the domain as a student, but they have also dedicated themselves to the academic side of the communication discipline. Their daily work has been to teach others about communication, to write about its complexities and its beauty, and to serve in ways that embody its principles. The communication professorate is faithful to both the discipline and its ideals. The term "communication professorate," then, encompasses the many roles of a professor: the scholar, the teacher, the servant, the thinker, the writer, the learner, as well as the advocate and the practitioner. Not all of these roles may be expressed as strongly, but they are nevertheless present. In the same way that a tennis player's forehand may be stronger than their backhand, a communication professor might be a stronger scholar than a teacher. But, the communication professor still engages in both. The professors in this study excelled in many areas: many of them are outstanding teachers, accomplished researchers, and serve at all levels: their department, their college, their university, and their professional organizations. Most importantly, they have been engaged in the communication discipline for over 25 years.

The project of this book is to describe the nature of the communication professorate. How does the communication professorate think? How does their thinking change and develop over the lifespan? How have they changed as a teacher in the course of their career? What ideas or theoretical constructs have made an impact on the way they understand their field of study? What has happened to them as people? I also ask: How do communication professors communicate? What do they pay attention to and what do they value? In seeking answers to these questions, the book reveals the common core that connects all students of human communication and invites each of us to reach out and make contact.

To date, society knows very little about the lives of those responsible for educating its members about communication. Until this volume, the communication professorate itself also knew very little about itself other than perhaps ad hoc anecdotes shared at conferences. This volume offers a description of the communication professorate for all those whose lives have been, and are, touched and shaped to varying degrees by the communication professorate. This includes students of communication, especially those who aspire to join the professorate, all those who read the work of the communication professorate, as well as the professorate itself.

This book, then, is for communication teachers and students, for professionals of communication, and even for those who want to learn to communicate better. It is also for scholars who want to understand how disciplinary thinking forms and changes, as well as for those who are interested in human development across the lifespan. For communication students and young professors, this book will show the journey ahead—its curvature and movement. It will illuminate the path and encourage persistence over the long term.

This first chapter accomplishes two major goals. First, I give theoretical context for the study, focusing specifically on human development over the lifespan. Second, I detail the overall study, providing background on participants, how research was conducted, and how the data were analyzed. In the conclusion of this chapter, I provide a roadmap for the book.

Theoretical Background

The study of human development grew in the field of psychology. In the 1950s, Jean Piaget (1952) outlined how children developed through time and pointed out that adults and children simply think differently. Children, he exposed, progress through distinctive stages of cognitive development; from a sensory-motor stage to the ability to think abstractly (formal operations). Piaget's theory was groundbreaking because it showed that children's thinking and actions develop through time and are slowly acquired. But, of course, Piaget's model stopped in adolescence, even though people continue to develop throughout their lifespan.

In *Childhood and Society*, Erikson (1950) extended Piaget's model by looking at the whole picture of human growth. In his work, he outlined eight stages for the development of man. From birth until death, each person sorts through a unique set of psychological crises, which will either prevent normal growth, or, if resolved, will enable the individual to develop in a healthy way. In infancy (0 to 1.5 years), the child is sensing trust or mistrust in the environment, in the people caring for him/her, and in himself. As Erikson wrote, "the firm establishment of enduring patterns for the solution of the nuclear conflict of basic trust versus basic mistrust in mere existence is the first task of the ego, and thus first of all a task for maternal care" (pp. 219–220). In early childhood, the child faces the tension between autonomy and shame, which is strongly influenced by parental responses to the child's behavior, such as encouragement or criticism. Between the ages of 3 and 5, the child resolves the tension between initiative and guilt. If managed successfully, the child will focus on their own competency from about 5 years old to 12 years. During this stage, she will confront her abilities to learn, to solve problems, to succeed, and to fail. In the process, the child will either develop a sense of competence, formally called industry, or will feel inferiority. From this stage, the individual moves into adolescence, defined here as between the ages of 12 to 18 years old. Erickson described this transition well:

> With the establishment of a good relationship to the world of skills and tools, and with the advent of sexual maturity, childhood proper comes to an end. Youth begins....the growing and developing youths, faced with this physiological revolution within them, are now primarily concerned with what they appear to be in the eyes of others as compared with what they feel they are, and with the question of how to connect the roles and skills cultivated earlier. (p. 261)

Adolescence then confronts the individual with his or her own identity. "Who am I," she or he will ask. "Who will I become?" If these questions are answered, the adolescent will confirm his or her role. If not, they might experience "role confusion." As young people master their identity, they move to the next stage: to build relationships with others, to explore commitment to another person, and to create a family. Between the ages of 18 through 40 years old, the person seeks to overcome isolation and moves toward successful intimacy. During middle age (40–65 years), the individual faces generativity or stagnation. Generativity, Erikson explained, is "the interest in establishing and guiding the next generation" or a "parental kind of responsibility" (p. 231). "Where this enrichment fails," Erikson wrote, "a regression from generativity to an obsessive need for pseudo intimacy … takes places." Finally, in older age, above 65 years old, the person seeks to reconcile their accomplishments, their journey, as well as accept death without fear. In the last stage, thus, the individual either finds integrity in their own life or experiences despair.

Erikson's stages of human development across the lifespan point to a person's ability to solve psychological tensions and crises. Other theorists have sought to describe human growth. Abraham Maslow's work is a case in point.

Maslow (1971) captured human growth without a time frame. Instead, he proposed that human growth was directed toward self-actualization—the process of making progression choices rather than regression choices. People, he wrote, "are always both actuality and potentiality" (p. 41). Self-actualization is the striving toward potentiality; a person's engagement in that life-long process *is* growth. Maslow's infamous hierarchy of needs presents those needs in a hierarchical order. First, the individual needs to meet basic *physiological needs* such as breathing, food, water, sex, and excretion. When those needs are met, *safety needs* become important: body, employment, resources, property, and health. In the third level of the pyramid are love and the *need to belong*. This is where our need for friendship, family, and intimacy can be met. The fourth layer focuses on *esteem needs*. To move toward self-actualization, the individual needs self-esteem, confidence, respect by others, and respect of others. On top of the pyramid sits self-actualization: the process of self-acceptance, of engagement in progression choices, that is, behaviors that care for the self, an increasing lack of prejudice, and an enactment of creative potential. For Maslow, then, human development was the project of realizing one's potential.

Human development, viewed from the perspective of psychologists, involves reconciling inner tensions, moving toward one's potential, and successfully solving contradictory pulls. From the perspective of sociology, a person's life cannot be separated from the context in which the individual lives. Historical time and place matter. They affect and constrain a person's choices, ways of thinking, and the opportunities that they might have. This claim is the central premise of Life Course Theory, a perspective that has emerged from several longitudinal studies.

Life Course Theory proposes several central claims that can be summarized as follows. First, and as Elder (1998) explained, "the life course of individuals is embedded in and shaped by the historical times and places they experience over their lifetime" (p. 3). Second, "the developmental impact of a succession of life transitions or events is contingent on when they occur in a person's life" (p. 3). Third, people's individual lives are linked to the social networks in which they are embedded. Elder expressed this third principle in this way: "lives are lived interdependently, and social and historical influences are expressed through this network of shared relationships" (p. 4). But, of course, in spite of historical, contextual, and relational links, individuals can nevertheless respond. "Individuals" Elder wrote, "construct their own life course through the choices and actions they take within the opportunities and constraints of history and social circumstances" (p. 4). From the perspective of Life Course Theory, then, human development cannot be separated from the social and historical context in which the individual operates; opportunities sometimes arise not as a result of serendipity but from a larger social force that makes such opportunities possible in the first place.

Human development across the lifespan is only just getting underway for communication researchers. One person leading this movement is Jon Nussbaum, who is one of the participants in this study. In his work, Nussbaum and his colleagues have developed a lifespan perspective that challenges common assumptions that are dominant in other theoretical approaches (e.g., Nussbaum & Baringer, 2000; Nussbaum & Friedrich, 2005). Theoretically, Nussbaum draws on five assertions. First, the lifespan perspective "rejects commonly accepted notions of almost universal decline as we age" (Nussbaum & Friedrich, 2005, p. 584). There are, according to Nussbaum, "many differences between normal, optimal, and pathological aging" (Nussbaum & Baringer, 2000, p. 201). Some aspects of a person's behaviors or thinking may decline, but some aspects may not. Learning and growth can occur at any time. This is well illustrated by George Vaillant's (2012) *Harvard Grant Study*, which followed 264 men throughout their lives. One of the key findings of the study is that some individuals' best contributions occurred much later in life in their '80s and '90s. "Each of us," Nussbaum (Nussbaum & Baringer, 2000) wrote, "can optimize our chances for good health and communication across the life span" (p. 201).

The second assertion is that "development in various behaviors may occur at different times with different speed" (Nussbaum & Friedrich, 2005, p. 584). Consider, for instance, speaking a second language. At first, the learning may be very slow as the person acquires basic vocabulary. As the vocabulary increases and the use of verbs becomes more fluid, the person might be able to learn additional words more quickly. At the same time, it might take years for this individual to get close to the accent of a native speaker—to use a similar rate of speech or intonation. However, that same person's writing ability might be much stronger than their ability to speak the language. Learning a second language, then, is a life-long journey, and the skills required to speak a second language fluently will develop at different times with different speed. For Nussbaum and his colleagues, that assertion applies to human development across the lifespan.

The third assertion is that "development is best viewed as a gain-loss dynamic" (Nussbaum & Friedrich, 2005, p. 584). Movement and learning in one direction may also be related to losses in another direction. Sometimes, this might occur simultaneously. To build on the previous example, and to speak from my own experience, as a person develops the ability to speak a second language fluently, they might simultaneously lose some of their ability to speak their native tongue. In the same way that they searched for words early on in the second language, they might now be searching for words in their native tongue. Speaking a second language is a gain, but it also involves a loss. The lifespan perspective emphasizes this point: "aging throughout the life span can be described as a dynamic process that balances gains and losses" (Nussbaum & Baringer, 2000, p. 202).

The fourth assertion is that "there is much intra- and inter- individual diversity throughout the life span" (Nussbaum & Friedrich, 2005, p. 584). Not everyone will age in the same way. There will be differences in spite of general similarities. Professionally, for instance, some individuals may peak early on while others shine later on in life. In one article, Malcolm Gladwell (2008) challenged the notion that we equate genius with precocity. As he explained, "Doing something truly creative, we're inclined to think, requires the freshness and exuberance and energy of youth" (para. 6). There is evidence to promote this thinking: Mozart, T.S. Eliot, Herman Melville, and Picasso all accomplished greatness in their '20s. But some were late bloomers. In his article, Gladwell described the path of Cézanne. Gladwell wrote: "If you go to the Cézanne room at the Musée D'Orsay, in Paris—The finest collection of Cézanne in the world—the array of masterpieces you'll find along the back wall were all painted at the end of his career" (para. 9). The point is that some of us are like Picasso and some of us are more like Cézanne. Every person has his or her own journey and will develop differently across the lifespan.

Finally, the lifespan perspective "assumes that the person and the environment are engaged in a transactional relationship, influencing and being influenced by each other" (Williams & Nussbaum, 2013, p. 6). This aspect of the theory echoes the key principles of Life Course Theory, but it also points out that the relationships between and among people help to contribute to the meaning of the context that surrounds them. A person affects the environment, but also other people. The lifespan perspective "suggests that relationships, rather than objects or elements, are of central importance" (p. 6).

The lifespan perspective is useful because it foregrounds communication processes. It proposes principles of human development that extend and encompass previous theoretical frameworks. This project is informed by the theoretical landscape of scholars on human development across the lifespan. But it will also push its boundaries by focusing on how a person grows with an academic discipline. The study asks: what disciplinary knowledge (e.g., concepts, theories, and ideas) affects the way practitioners of that discipline think and act? In what ways do the individual's thinking and actions become the object of study itself?

To use an analogy, the best tennis player in the world is Roger Federer—winner of a total of 17 Grand Slams. Roger Federer is fit; he has strong leg muscles, a slim body type, weighs 187 pounds, and is over 6 feet tall. Of course, Roger has had a great impact on the game and many consider him to be the best in history. But, if you look closely at his arms and compare his right arm and his left arm, you'll notice that his right arm is much bigger than his left arm, which is the result of using a one-handed forehand and backhand. He has made his mark on the game of tennis, but playing tennis has also morphed his body, distorting it one way rather than another, creating aspects of his body to match the demands of the sport. This book's project is to show how the communication discipline has affected its own participants—how their ways of thinking and acting, their values and their talk, have slowly made them communication professionals.

The Project

In the spring of 2014, I enrolled in a course titled "Methods of Thinking" taught by Dr. Jay Raphael, professor and chair of Theater Arts at the University of Arkansas at Little Rock. The premise of the course was to examine how various professionals would think through a problem or a task, and what knowledge they brought to bear to engage in some activity. One Friday, Jay brought in a chef, the next week it was an architect, a historian, and a philosopher. We met with an orchestra conductor and a sculptor. At every class, he would ask the guest to speak about their ways of thinking: "What is it like to think like a historian?" or "How does a sculptor think through a problem?" From this course emerged my own question about what a professional of communication would bring to the table. How does a communication professional see the world? How do they solve problems? What knowledge from their discipline gives them vision or understanding? And how do they communicate in their own lives?

To put it differently, imagine you are looking at the sky with an astronomer. All of us can look up, but few of us know more than the Big Dipper and the Little Dipper, and the beauty of the moon. But an astronomer would be able to see patterns in the sky that we would not be able to decipher. They would have information about the stars and planets that would be much more complex than our understanding of it. Expertise provides a way of seeing the world. One key question for this project is: what can a communication pro-fessor see, hear, and understand that other people may not pay attention to?

This question was the starting point. It led to many other questions, most of which were about development and growth. I became interested in figur-ing out how a person's disciplinary thinking changes. How does it mature? What does it move from and to? And what happens over the lifespan. How does a discipline change a person? What lessons can be learned from their journey and development? But, I also wanted to know how they practiced communication. In every discipline, the professorate did something beyond simply thinking: they acted in the world in particular ways. So, how does someone who studies and thinks about communication engage in it? What do they value? What behaviors do they believe are crucial? Is there some form of consensus that exists among communication scholars? Is there a core way of thinking and a core way of acting?

To answer these many questions, I developed a semi-structured interview schedule (see Appendix A). In the first part of the interview, I asked "easy" questions to get to know participants. I asked why they chose the field of communication, what drew them to it, and what they loved about it today. The core of the interview probed into their development. I asked about the differences in how they approached the classroom across time, what signifi-cant turning points they experienced in the way they think about commu-nication, and what ideas or constructs informed their thinking. I then asked about the way they practice communication, probing as deeply as I could in how they engage with others, as well as what they pay attention to when they communicate at home or at work. In the conclusion, I asked them to map their journey so far into stages and to share any advice they would give to students about how to communicate well. These questions, as well as others that emerged, guided the interview process.

For this project, Kristina Godfrey, Amanda Pasierb (two graduate students at the University of Arkansas at Little Rock), and I interviewed 30 faculty members across the nation. Each faculty member had to meet two key criteria: (a) they had to have earned a PhD in Communication, and (b) they had to have been an active faculty member for at least 25 years. The focus was not necessarily on selecting faculty who were "stars" of the discipline, although many of them are, in fact, well-known (see Appendix B for the list of partici-pants). Faculty who were active in teaching, research, or service qualified for the project. The main prerogative was to interview faculty members who had engaged in deep thinking, teaching, reflecting, and writing about communication throughout their lifespan. These participants reflect variety across areas of study—from rhetoric, mass communication, interpersonal communication, meta-theory, nonverbal communication, to gender studies. They also come from 22 different universities in the US: from the University of Washington, down to the University of Arizona, east to George Mason University, and everywhere in between.

The interviews lasted on average 45 minutes, with some being shorter (about 35 minutes) to some lasting up to 90 minutes. All of the interviews were audio-recorded. Most of them were conducted over the phone, although when it was possible, the interview was done in person or via Skype. For example, I interviewed one participant as he drove through Little Rock to visit Ohio during winter break. After conducting the interviews, they were transcribed to reproduce on paper what was said during the interview. We transcribed for words and content, and not for details that would be common in the study of language and social interaction, conversation analysis, or discourse analysis. My graduate students (at the time), Kristina and Amanda, both drew on the data set to write master's projects. The process of working together on the data and the analysis of their data selection began the process of thematic analysis, reflection, and implications.

As Braun and Clark (2006) defined it, thematic analysis "is a method for identifying, analyzing, and reporting matters (themes) within data" (p. 79). Traditionally, thematic analysis can begin either with the data or from theory—inductively or deductively. For this project, I chose to let the data speak and to allow the themes from the study to emerge. Most of the chapters are written with an inductive framework: the findings emerged from listening to the voices of our participants and appeared until we reached saturation—which began to emerge around the 20th interview. I followed the traditional process of thematic analysis, which, as described by Braun and Clark, includes (a) familiarizing yourself with the data, (b) generating initial codes, (c) searching for themes, (d) reviewing themes, (e) defining and naming the themes, and (f) producing the report. Chapter 8 is one exception. In writing that chapter, I applied my model of positive communication (see Mirivel, 2014) to the data to see how it aligns with the communication behaviors that communication scholars valued. In that sense, I used the model to code the interviews and direct the analysis. Overall, then, the project is grounded in thematic analysis, a process that involves "searching across a data set…to find repeated patterns of meaning (p. 86)."

Beyond the methods, engaging in conversation with these communication scholars was a life lesson in itself. Throughout the process, we were surrounded by the voices of 30 experienced mentors, each with their own perspectives and advice. I hope the rest of this book showcases their stories and has the same positive impact on others that it had on me. With this project in mind, consider the direction and content of the book.

Our Road Map

In this book, I argue that communication competency is a slow, gradual awakening toward others. Communicating well is a lifelong process, not a state of being. To support this claim, the chapters in this book reveal where today's communication professorate got their start, how their thinking has changed over the course of their career, and the directions they have taken in the process of growing as a professor and communicator.

In Chapter 2, I focus on the commonalities across our participants. I explore some of their shared experiences, the ways of thinking that were common in the interviews, and what binds them together as a group. Grounded in literature on the nature of the professorate, the chapter reveals that many communication professionals began their journey with a natural sensitivity to human interaction. Many of them were also shaped by childhood experiences that led them to choose communication as a discipline.

Chapter 3 is about how the communication professorate featured in this study grew. I draw on Carl Rogers (1961) and the way he described the process of becoming a person. Specifically, I show that our participants gradually awakened to themselves more fully. They slowly emerged from doubt and fear to self-confidence. And, as a result, they were able to move from thinking of themselves to thinking of others.

For all of our participants, students were at the core of their professorial career. Chapter 4 explores the nature of teaching excellence and the directions participants took as they evolved in the classroom. The chapter shows how communication professors consistently moved in the direction of students and their learning. They moved from speaking at students to listening deeply. Ultimately, it was the focus on students that gave meaning to their lives and their careers.

Chapter 5 is the heart of this book. There, I examine how communication professors' thinking evolved over the years. The chapter shows how slow learning truly is, and the years it takes to move from thinking about social reality in a dualistic way, to accept uncertainty, and to nevertheless take a stand. The biggest shift in disciplinary thinking was moving from the trans-mission model of communication to the constitutive view. Our participants were influenced by this disciplinary trend and thought of communication as a process of co-construction. And, of course, this changes everything.

Chapter 6 is about how disciplinary expertise shapes the way communica-tion professors see, hear, and experience the world. Studying communication gave our participants a lens through which to see and appreciate nonverbal behaviors in action, the use of language, and, unfortunately, a lot of missed opportunities for connection. Communication professors can see what people are doing, the problems they create and how communication can hurt, but they can also see the space for potential; where people could move in, lean in, and get closer.

Chapters 7 and 8 explore the same question: "How do communication professors communicate?" In answering this question, I first show the general movements that take place across the lifespan. Based on the interviews we conducted, I found that our participants moved toward an increasing sense of consciousness and mindfulness and that they incrementally listened more deeply, became gentler, and gave themselves the freedom to play with lan-guage and humor. In Chapter 8, the focus is on the communication behaviors they value. Listening, of course, is the most important, but so is being kind and affecting others positively. Communicating well is a process across the lifespan, but some behaviors should still be practiced.

Together, the chapters in this book describe the lives of today's communi-cation professorate—how they think, act, and live.

Conclusion

This book focuses on the lives of some of those who serve in the contemporary communication professorate: individuals who have spent the majority of their professional lives studying processes of human communication. Most of them have earned all of their degrees in this area of study; all of them have earned the highest degree possible in the study of communication. In addition, they have spent at least 25 years after their doctorate teaching, writing, serving, and speaking to others about the importance of communication. The rest of this book describes what the communication professorate can teach us about living that full life. It reveals the similarities across those scholars and what we can learn from each of them.

There is always a strange feeling when standing in front of a mirror looking at yourself. Even though the mirror can only precisely reflect your physical appearance, your perceptions, mood, self-esteem, or confidence will color what you see. There are, of course, the expectations in your mind. The image you have of yourself might not be reflected in what you see: you may feel younger, more bold, or fitter. Writing this book and interviewing scholars in my discipline was very much like looking in a mirror—I saw, to quote John Peters (1999), "the self in the other and the other in the self." I found pieces of me in many interviews; my ways of thinking and being became apparent, reflected back to me. I also found differences, but maybe those are the characteristics that I refused to see in myself.

References

Braun, V., & Clarke, V. (2006). Using thematic analysis in psychology. *Qualitative Research in Psychology, 3*(2), 77–101.

Elder, G. H., Jr. (1998). The life course as developmental theory. *Child Development, 69*(1), 1–12.

Erikson, E. H. (1950). *Childhood and Society.* New York, NY: Norton.

Gladwell, M. (2008, October 20). Late bloomers: Why do we equate genius with precocity? *The New Yorker.* Retrieved from http://www.newyorker.com/magazine/2008/10/20/late-bloomers-2.

Maslow, A. (1971). *The farther reaches of human nature.* New York, NY: Penguin.

Mirivel, J. C. (2014). *The art of positive communication: Theory and practice.* New York, NY: Peter Lang.

Nussbaum, J. F., & Baringer, D. K. (2000). Message production across the life-span: Communication and aging. *Communication Theory, 10*(2), 200–209.

Nussbaum, J. F., & Friedrich, G. (2005). Instructional/developmental communication: Current theory, research and future trends. *Journal of Communication, 55,* 578–593.

Peters, J. D. (1999). *Speaking into the air: A history of the idea of communication.* Chicago, IL: The University of Chicago Press.

Piaget, J. (1952). *The origins of intelligence in children* (Vol. 8, No. 5, pp. 18–1952). New York, NY: International Universities Press.

Rogers, C. (1961). *On becoming a person.* Boston, MA: Houghton Mifflin.

Vaillant, G. E. (2012). *Triumphs of experience: The men of the Harvard Grant Study.* Cambridge, MA: The Belknap Press of Harvard University Press.

· 2 ·

WHAT IS THE NATURE OF THE COMMUNICATION PROFESSORATE?

When I met Bill, I met my future. As a young sophomore in college, entering a 2000-level course in your chosen major was exciting. On the first day, Bill stood with pride, introduced the questions of the course, spoke with efficient tempo, moved in the classroom to reach students, and smiled often. As a communication professor, Bill's presence, standing well over 6 feet tall and wearing sneakers, jeans, and a polo, was influential. His gestures and speech were both precise and welcoming, especially when describing concepts. He was, quite simply, a great teacher.

Bill introduced me to the communication discipline and became my mentor. He led me through an independent study on the origins of language use, drove me through the landscape of Iowa to go fishing, listened to my thinking, and encouraged me to write every day no matter what. He was the first person I called when I received my GRE scores, and one year at the field's national convention, I drove 3 hours across the central coast in California to see him for one evening. From my perspective, Bill embodied what it meant to be a professor and a scholar. Now I am my own person, but for a long time, I just wanted to be like Bill.

Looking back, maybe Bill saw himself in me as much as I projected myself in him. We shared a common interest in ideas and were both curious about the complexity of human relationships. We both enjoyed sports and appreciated the boundaries of human excellence. We were also both foreigners of sorts—me as an international student from France and him as a U.S. citizen raised in Germany. We were decades apart in age and experience, but Bill and I shared a common core. We were more similar than different.

Much like Bill and I, the communication professors in this study are unique individuals with distinguishing experiences. But, in spite of their differences, the communication professors we studied have a lot in common. This chapter shows this common core. It answers these questions: What personal and professional experiences do participants have in common? What similarities do participants share about their journey, their experiences, the way they think, and about who they are as individuals? One major point of similarity is the fact that all participants are active or retired professors, so I start there and describe what professors actually do—their professional tasks and responsibilities. Then, I describe five common experiences that emerged from the interviews and reveal the heart of the communication professoriate. The chapter ends with a major point of difference between an aspiring student and a professor emeritus.

What Do Professors Do?

Today, most professors have three main responsibilities that are often placed in this order: they conduct research, teach students, and serve the university and the community. Often, these responsibilities were thought of as distinct domains of practice, until Ernest Boyer (1990) reconsidered the nature of scholarship and the priorities of the professoriate. In the book, Boyer asked fundamental questions about the nature of faculty and their work: (a) What does it mean to be a professor? (b) What priorities should guide the professoriate? And (c) what impact should professors have beyond themselves? With these questions, Boyer sought to provide "a more comprehensive, more dynamic understanding of scholarship" (p. 16), and introduced four interrelated functions to define a professor's work: the scholarship of discovery, the scholarship of integration, the scholarship of application, and the scholarship of teaching. Boyer's ideas are still influential today in defining the nature of the responsibilities of the professoriate and shaping its evolution.

The scholarship of discovery focuses on research and the advancement of knowledge. "Scholarly investigation," Boyer (1990) wrote, "is at the very heart of academic life, and the pursuit of knowledge must be assiduously cultivated and defended" (p. 18). One important function of a professor's work, then, is to contribute to the world of ideas, pursue answers to complex questions, and engage in the process of inquiry. With the scholarship of discovery, professors read actively in their discipline and beyond, tackle important questions, collect and analyze data, and publish their findings. They read, think, and write, and may discover new ideas along the way.

The scholarship of integration is the second function. It builds on the premise of discovery, but places the professor in a position to synthesize research findings in light of other disciplines. "By integration," Boyer (1990) argued, "we mean making connections across the disciplines, placing the specialties in larger contexts, [or] illuminating data in a revealing way" (p. 18). Here, the scholar is situated at the nexus of multiple disciplines, bridging differences with a common thread, and exhibiting what Gardner (2006) described as the mind of the future—the synthesizing mind.

The third form of scholarship Boyer (1990) described is the scholarship of application. This is the impulse to make a difference in society, which reflects the "principle that higher education must serve the interests of the larger community" (p. 22). Most faculty members, of course, engage in a variety of service roles. They may serve as graduate coordinators or on university councils. For Boyer, though, the scholarship of application is more than service or departmental citizenship. "To be considered scholarship," he explained, "service activities must be tied directly to one's special field of knowledge and relate to, and flow directly out of, this professional activity" (p. 22). The more a faculty member can find ways to affect practice with theory, and inform theory from solving practical problems, the more they are engaging in the scholarship of application.

The last element is the scholarship of teaching. With this label, Boyer (1990) sought to describe teaching as an art that involves fostering student learning, applying complex pedagogical principles, and finding ways to not only transmit knowledge, but also "transforming and extending it" (p. 24). The scholarship of teaching is the heart of academic work. As he wrote, "in the end, inspired teaching keeps the flame of scholarship alive…without the teaching function, the continuity of knowledge will be broken and the store of human knowledge dangerously diminished" (p. 24).

Boyer's call to the professoriate gave scholars and teachers a North Star for their career. In fact, much work has been published to support Boyer's proposal and to advance professors' understanding of how to do their work more effectively. For example, there are countless published studies on effective teaching in higher education (e.g., Bain, 2004; McKeachie & Svinicki, 2014; Palmer, 2007). There are many resources for faculty about how to do research—whether those are methodological guides (Lindlof & Taylor, 2011; Weber & Fuller, 2012) or guides about how to write and publish in academia (e.g., Haynes, 2010). And there are also books on how to practice "engaged scholarship" (e.g., Van de Ven, 2007) and studies of the professoriate generally (e.g., Wulff & Austin, 2004). Yet, we know very little about who professors are as people.

This is especially true in the field of communication studies. Here, scholars have synthesized the history of our field (Peters, 1999), organized domains of thought to give structure and meaning to our varied sub-disciplinary impulses (Craig, 1999), and shown how the field came together through influential scholars and their ideas (Rogers, 1994). Yet, and to my knowledge, we have not examined who we are as a group, how we are united by common values, what defines us, or what the personal and professional journey of developing as a communication professor is like. This chapter fills this gap by highlighting the common personal experiences that emerged from interviewing some of the most experienced professors in the field. I use this chapter to introduce most of our participants and show what communication professors are like. My hope is for us to see that we are more similar than different.

What Communication Professors Have in Common

Our interviews revealed five common experiences. First, our communication professors shared an affinity with communication and found a discipline that aligned with their natural strengths. Second, many of our participants were inherently sensitive and attentive to human interaction. Third, most studied communication to understand personal experiences, especially those that occurred in their childhood. Fourth, across their professional journey, they were all guided by curiosity and the drive to answer a lifelong question. Fifth, and perhaps more importantly, they were passionate about the discipline.

An Affinity With Communication

When I was a teenager in Switzerland, I was asked to give a presentation on Greek mythology. This was a difficult time in my life, as my parents did not get along, and my school work suffered. But for this presentation, something was different. I wanted to do well. I poured myself into the readings, developed a presentation, and delivered it. At the end of the talk, the teacher said "that's exactly what a good presentation looks like." She called on my classmates to move in that direction. That speech saved my grade for that course, but more importantly, in that moment, I flirted with one of my strengths; I touched a natural ability of sorts that could be capitalized on. This experience took place many years before I learned English as a second language in the US, or became a student in the Department of Communication at the University of Northern Iowa, or studied public speaking, or even realized that I would be engaging in the study and practice of human communication. But there it was, a moment in time in which I experienced a natural strength. My experience, it turns out, matches the experiences of many communication professionals.

Steven Beebe is one example. Dr. Beebe is a Distinguished Professor of Communication Studies and the author of several textbooks used in class-rooms around the world. Among the list of his great accomplishments, in 2013 he served as president of the National Communication Association, the largest professional communication association in the world. In the interview, he explained what drew him to the field. "My first major was music," he said, "but I realized I also had *an affinity to communication*, public speaking those kinds of things." He added, "My *original attraction* [emphasis added] was the fact that I could give speeches, and people could and would listen, and I could hold their attention so that element of the performance aspect of the communication first interested me."

Tom Socha's experience was strikingly similar. Professor Socha, university professor at Old Dominion University and founding editor of the *Journal of Family Communication*, remembered: "I started out as an undergraduate, my first major was music and I really was interested in music." Then, he explained, "I had a great experience with a professor at Loyola University in Chicago who convinced me that communication sort of fell in between my interest in music and business and that I should do more with that." Tom became a communication major shortly after that experience, but later in the interview, he acknowledged a key moment:

> When I was in 8th grade, we had a teacher who was interested in oral communica-
> tion, public speaking, so she had us doing exercises and things in class and those
> came easy to me. Those were fun things to do, where other people seemed to strug-
> gle, to be concerned, I just never struggled, it just came pretty easily and naturally
> to me.

Many scholars I spoke to also had an interest in music. Music, after all, is a form of expression, a way of communicating. But music was not the center point of their affinity. Communication was. Public speaking was. Or, as in the case of Kristine Muñoz, professor at the University of Iowa and author of several books on culture and language and social interaction, it was writing. When I asked her to describe what drew her to the field, she explained:

> The immodest part is, I was good at it. And I grew up not someone who was very good at many things (laughs). I was good at writing and I was good at Spanish and that was about it. And in graduate school those two things came together. And then there was teaching and I was good at that too. And those were the three things in my life that I would have to say, those might be the only things that I would ever claim to have been good at it so once I found them there was no reason to look any further.

Most communication professors discovered an affinity with the discipline—with its demands, with its values, or even with its tasks. They found an alignment with their identity and their strengths and saw an opportunity to bring those strengths to bear and to take, as Kristine explained, the "path of least resistance." John Daly, Regents Professor of the University of Texas System and Distinguished Scholar from the National Communication Association, echoed this point, saying that communicating well came "easy to him" and that scholarship was a game he could win at. Similarly, Em Griffin, professor emeritus at Wheaton College and author of the popular *A First Look at Communication Theory*, gave a speech and thought to himself, "There is power here, speech or communication can be effective."

Sometimes, as is the case for Allan Ward, civil rights activist and professor emeritus at the University of Arkansas at Little Rock, it was a matter of finding it:

> And so when I got to college I had never heard of the communication field, but as I started taking the Gen Ed classes that were required someone told me "you know when I hear you talk about what you are concerned about you need to take a communication course." And I said, "what's that?" And he said, "let me walk you over here." And he went over to that department and looked at the schedule and it started to sound like the questions that I have been saying would be answered to the things that I was wondering. So I signed up for my first course, the introduction to communication, and it was like I'd come home to the home I didn't know existed.

For many scholars, and just like my student Lacie, who I wrote about in Chapter 1, experiencing courses in communication was like finding a home. The discipline became the discursive space of their development and growth, the meeting of their strengths, and the point of reflection in which they saw who they were and who they might become. Finding the communication discipline was finding a safe space to explore ideas and thoughts, to think and write, to make contact, and to find the self.

In the 1990s I found myself in an introduction course at the University of Northern Iowa. In the course, we explored interpersonal communication, group communication, and, of course, public speaking. Ten years after my Greek Mythology speech, I was now experiencing again the joy of being in front of an audience, of sharing a message, and of thinking about the complexities of human connection. I too found a home away from home.

An Appropriate Sensitivity to Human Interaction

Allan Ward is professorial. His white hair is thinning, his torso leaning forward, and his enthusiasm is boundless. He often wears khakis, leather shoes, a button-up shirt, and a corduroy vest. There is a spring in his step and purpose. Allan Ward is everywhere: a luncheon on campus, an event at the library, a board meeting in downtown Little Rock, a get-together to honor alumni, or a small concert. Wherever I go, I see him there— involved in the community, bringing people together, and making contact.

In looking back at his experiences, Allan Ward, who, in spite of retirement, still teaches adult education courses across Arkansas, found a unique sensitivity to interaction. He didn't have a word for it, a descriptive, or a way of understanding it. The only word that came to describe it was "hypersensitive":

> I found as a child I was hypersensitive to how people were addressing each other talking to each other and I can remember that in grade school having all—I didn't have words for it but why did kids that I knew that I would be in their houses, their parents would talk to them and they would talk to their parents and I think, why do they do this? Why can't they, and I didn't have regular words, but why can't they talk normally and kindly and sincerely to each other? And I found the same on the playground at school in grade school.

Much later on, Allan would join a communication program, study semantics, and become active in the Civil Rights Movement, bringing people with perceived differences together, and see the power of dialogic communication for overcoming those perceived differences. But the sensitivity to the way that people engage with one another never left him—a force that many communication professionals shared. In my interview with Karen Foss, professor emeritus, Presidential Teaching Fellow, and former chair of the Department of Communication and Journalism at the University of New Mexico, she described her experience as a "calm," "quiet," and "powerful" energy. A grounded interest that is "always there." But the noticing was still very much the same. In one story, Karen shared a moment watching a couple's conflict during dinner unfold while her and her partner ate close to them:

> I remember my husband and I were sitting at a restaurant once and the couple next to us was, you know, they clearly lived together, she made a comment about not wanting him to play in this band or something and it could have been a very sort of simple kind of conversation but in the next 45 minutes that whole relationship unraveled and I wanted to walk over and say "Stop! Stop! Back up, start over!" [laughter] but it was just so incredible and so horrible to listen to, you know? So I just think that people do not think about communication choices and I think that we as communication professionals do.

Many communication professors noticed the details in human conversations and saw how they could unfold differently. They experienced the ability to see the interactional problems, and sometimes the hate that people produced, knowing full well that they could do it better—more lovingly. This was well displayed in Tom Socha's story, whose focus has been on family communication and parenting. "I hear a lot of stories about bad parenting," he said during the interview. "I cringe," he added, "more when I hear people saying just horrible things, you know like, I think, 'Oh there is so much better way you could have put that' or 'this is another 15 ways you might want to say it' or 'is there a better way to do that?'"

A sensitivity to communication emerged as a natural trait that was also nurtured by the discipline. In his interview, John Peters, the A. Craig Baird Professor at the University of Iowa, who also wrote the thought-breaking book *Speaking Into the Air*, said: "I think I am really sensitive to speech acts. I think I really notice when people are doing things with words. I think that most people don't realize, always, how they're operating with words. I think that that's something that's not helpful." Dan O'Hair, professor and interim senior vice provost at the University of Kentucky, in a similar vein, expressed that communication professors are "hypersensitive to all of the things that we have learned about human behavior from a communication perspective." And Gary Kreps, the University Distinguished Professor and chair of the Department of Communication at George Mason University, said, "I'm very sensitive to those different factors that are usually invisible to other people that either can promote good communication or not."

By definition, hypersensitivity refers to being "excessively or abnormally sensitive." For many communication professors and students, the word may not resonate. On the one hand, it is a strength—a unique sense of what is right or wrong in everyday communicative events or even a skill in perception. Being abnormal is not inherently a problem—it simply means that a person is outside of the norm. In fact, communication professors are not normal. Aside from being highly educated in the discipline, they see, hear, feel, and understand human interaction in sensible ways. On the other hand, and as Kristine Muñoz, whose latest writing explored the many dimensions of silence, taught me in our interview, the term implies that the problem lies within us. I interviewed Kristine much later on in the project, so I asked her: "Is the word resonating with you in some way and if so, how?"

> Yes, and I would say although it suggests that, I mean hypersensitive. I would say we are appropriately sensitive. Sometimes I walk around thinking there are a lot of people in the world who are tone deaf to the impact that they are having or the things that they don't notice. They say this and they do that and they must think that that is okay, and it's so not. An example I'll give just to get away from age and gender. I had a colleague who said, described herself as, "I do have a short fuse." Now this is somebody who would be screaming at you across the table at a committee meeting from one minute to the next and then the next day act like nothing had happened. And when she said I do have a short fuse, I was just dumbstruck and it's like "Oh, so you think it is alright to do that, you do not think this is a problem." So it is like saying we are hyper-considerate because we do not scream at people when we are angry. I think the people who do not hear the racism and the sexism and what they say are the hypo-sensitive, it condenses the problem.

Communication professors might be hypersensitive or maybe others around us are "tone deaf." Perhaps, there is a more positive frame. In my conversation with Karen Foss, she also took issue with the term "hypersensitive." This is not surprising; her collaboration with an art therapist is drawing on colors to uplift people and to move beyond binary thinking. She said to me,

> I would never use that term, even though we are maybe getting at the same things. When I think of communication visually I see it as grounded and down below in the background so the hypersensitivity term does not resonate. It feels too fanatic.

I probed more deeply to gain suggestions. Karen replied with "I might use the term 'grounded,' I might use 'powerful.'" She explained it more deeply:

> Well if I think about communication interaction and I am thinking, I mean I am being aware of communication, it's more like it is sitting there for me to draw from and make use of and bring to the conversation but it is … it is funny, I have this very clear sense of it but it is hard to describe. It's calm and it's quiet and it's powerful in the background as a resource I can draw on.

Now, hypersensitivity is energy and a strength. In the most positive frame, which emerged from Tom Socha, it is mindfulness. Tom, who is leading the positive communication movement in the field of communication, said to me:

> Instead of sensitivity, I would say mindfulness, for me, you know? Sensitivity would mean that I am more open to communicative processes in the world and more attentive to them. But some I ignore, like everybody else. …I am more mindful of the communication around me and increasing my mindfulness puts me in that context. So I am a participant in those exchanges but it also connects me to other discourses better there at that moment, you know? I become more mindful ….And I think the idea that studying communication makes you more mindful about communication processes. I think that is a fundamental goal of all communication courses.

Whether you conceive of it as mindfulness or hypersensitivity, the communication scholars I interviewed reflected an awareness of both the way communication was unfolding in the present moment and what was possible—what could be done and sometimes what should be done. The sense of what could be was reflected both inward and outward. They saw potentiality in other's discourses, but also noticed that they could communicate more effectively themselves, even though, as Gary Kreps explained, "Sometimes I am not always receptive to the ways I am communicating as I am to observing others."

Participants' sensitivity to the power of communication—the way it affects people, their potential, the relationships, and social realities, gave them both a great deal of appreciation for minute slices of human interaction as well as triggering personal reflection on how they have not met their own personal ideals about how to communicate well. There is a constant realization that they could have communicated differently. Once you recognize the power of communication, it is difficult to ignore that it could be done more effectively.

Influential Childhood Experiences

In many cases, communication professors studied communication from experiences that emerged in childhood or from facing challenges that they needed an answer for. In my own experience, I struggled to see my parents interact in their marriage and found it painful to see the way they handled conflict. On one occasion I remember seeking to bring everyone to the table after a violent interaction. I cooked dinner and tried to bring peace back to the household. There is no doubt that this experience marked me, but that there was inside of me a desire for more positive family interactions. In my teens, I traveled to the US without being able to speak English, and learned it by staying with a host family for 1 year, staying silent for many months. The inability to communicate, the confrontation of a large communication problem, certainly influenced my path. Many communication scholars spoke to childhood experiences or their past to make sense of their development and growth, including the choice to study communication and pursue a career in the discipline. I did not probe deeply into childhood experiences; it was not the function of the interview, nor was I prepared to explore it in depth with well-known scholars in the discipline. However, the professors I interviewed naturally spoke somewhat softly and hesitantly of those moments. This section reveals the importance that childhood experiences play in shaping future career paths.

Early in my interview with Art Bochner, I asked why he chose the field of communication. Dr. Bochner is the Distinguished University Professor at the University of South Florida, a past president of the National Communication Association, and leader of the autoethnographic movement in the field. In developing his answers, he explained that he started with biology, moved to English, and that through a serendipitous encounter moved into communication. Yet, at the end of the narrative, he said, "If I were to answer the question most directly, it is that I wanted to understand my own family and its communication. That's what really started me on a life committed to communication research and communication teaching."

Understanding family interaction, or being influenced by it, lies at the heart of many professors. In her answer to a similar question, Valerie Manusov, professor at the University of Washington, whose expertise focuses on nonverbal communication, hinted at it early on in her narrative. She first explained that in high school, she was already "interested in how people formed relationships." A few utterances later, in the middle of her stories, she added, "And so I think, you know, I tended to have not very good communication in my life that I found it really interesting from my personal perspective." Having heard this small statement, I probed more deeply at the end of her turn, in the middle of a longer pause, and asked her "What do you think really drew you to the field when you reflect back on it today?" This is what she said:

You know I had a pretty functional family but there were still enough difficulties about communication. I felt that there was so much that was kind of left unsaid and it was very consequential. I would watch my parents who were married until my mom passed at 45 years, but they really struggled with their own communication. So I think a lot of it was just that really personal level, like I just saw how important it was, but how hard it was and I think it must have been pretty complicated. So I think a lot of it had to do really with that very personal thing that I just …. . I wanted to understand it.

The search for understanding or answers about one's own experiences, particularly those that occurred in family interactions, were common. For example, Dawn O. Braithwaite, Willa Cather Professor and chair of the Department of Communication Studies at the University of Nebraska at Lincoln, explained, "I was with a stepfamily starting in junior high. My mother had died, my father remarried. I was in a very difficult stepfamily. So this idea of communication and the need of communication, really resonated with me." In fact, Dawn, who also led the National Communication Association as president, saw a poster during this time in her life that she still remembers today. She said, "I remember seeing this poster in my junior high classroom that was in a telephone advertisement and it said, 'Communication is the beginning of understanding.'"

Scholars, after all, often follow their passion, their questions, and seek to find answers to explain their experiences. Family interactions were sometimes problematic— fraught with conflict, challenges, or alcoholism, but sometimes positive experiences in family life prepared scholars for the communication discipline. In my interview with Tom Socha, he described his experiences at the family dinner table as being key for his development, memories of childhood that very much aligned with my experiences too:

I have thought about this too, I would say early on in my family, we spent quite a bit of time debating my father. My dad, he graduated from Loyola with a business degree, worked in the glass industry in Chicago his whole career, very pragmatic guy. Everything had to be like "So, how are we going to pay for this? And why are you doing this? And what is this communication stuff?" My middle brother chose social work as his field of study and my dad was like "Really? And how much money do you think you can make doing this?" Very, very pragmatic. So we had a lot of debate in our household over the dinner table. I had two brothers, so it was my two brothers and I and my father. And my mother would be there, she would sort of listen and sometimes would weigh in. But it was mostly this intellectual challenge at our family dinner table that honed my argumentation skills that honed my orientation towards communication.

In my interview with Wendy Leeds-Hurwitz, professor emerita at the University of Wisconsin at Parkside and director of the Center for Intercultural

Dialogue of the Council of Communication Associations, she grounded her interest in culture:

> I was very interested in studying interaction, I think the fact that I grew up in a family where one parent was born in the US and the other one was not. One parent was from Western Europe, the other was not. One parent ... . Both parents were fluent in multiple languages and I grew up in Washington, D.C., which has a very large international community, many of whom were family friends, my parents knew people in the embassies and the Foreign Service and so I grew up understanding that Americans were only one of many possibilities and that was not necessarily the case for everybody.

Sometimes, family life directly fostered the skills that would be needed later on. Arvind Singhal, who serves as the Samuel Shirley and Edna Holt Martson Endowed Professor in the Department of Communication at University of Texas at El Paso, said his grandfather played a crucial role in shaping his ability to write and to be creative.

> My grandfather, my father's father, retired when I was maybe five years old and he was a school teacher, college teacher, professor and my father was the only son so he came and began to live with us and that was I think one of the most wonderful things that happened to me in my childhood because he was professorial and he was grandfatherly. He created an incentive system for his three grandkids which included me as the youngest which was if we wrote a page in Hindi on any topic of our interest at age 5 and a page of English on any topic of my choice in cursive and if I solved 10 math problems that he would, age appropriate, he would give me a little monetary incentive and he would give me my two dollars of monetary incentive. And I don't think for a single day we missed that, so when you're 5 years old and your imagination begins to run wild on a piece of paper you develop a love for language and you develop a love for stories.

Arvind's story is just another example of how early childhood experiences shaped his trajectory. For Teri Thompson, professor at the University of Dayton, editor of *Health Communication* for over 20 years, and award-winning teacher, it was a life-changing moment with her brother. Perhaps the most poignant story came from Allan Ward's experience in the schoolyard.

> One child from a family that had come from Germany and he had a bit of an accent and this was during the Second World War and Germans were the enemy and so a group of guys, grade school students, waited around and hid after school and he was coming out and they grabbed him. They tied him to a tree in the middle of the schoolyard, they stripped him, they urinated on him, they defecated on him, and stoned him, and his family disappeared that night and were never heard from again.

In that moment, I interrupted: "This was in the community where you lived?" Allan answered:

> Yes, it was in the grade school grounds in that community. It was a walk from school not a school bus thing. We are talking third or fourth grade and … . I thought why do people, there's got to be another way. Well that just brought it so vividly home that I thought this kid is in our class, we are with him every day. How could there suddenly be this change to do these horrible things to him? What's this going to do to him forever? I just grasped for words or concept and so my propensity towards communication I didn't have, I'd say why don't people talk to each other? Why don't they talk to each other more gently?

Allan's story was not the norm in the interviews we conducted, but his final question was common—if not expressed directly, reflected in the way communication scholars thought. Why don't people talk to each other more kindly? Why don't people talk to each more gently at home? Or at work? Or in the school yard? Or in a faculty meeting? Perhaps, our sense of common purpose stems from seeking to answer these basic questions.

When I joined the graduate program at the University of Colorado at Boulder, my first course was with Robert Craig, Distinguished Scholar from the National Communication Association and past president of the International Communication Association. One of our tasks was to write a review of literature on a topic of our choosing. I chose to review the work on conflict. In a side conversation with one of the newest assistant professors Timothy Kuhn, he asked about my topic: "What did you choose for you review?" "Conflict," I said with assurance. "Do you have a sense of why you chose it?" The truth is that I didn't really know. "I just find it interesting." "Often," he added, "we choose a topic that is connected to us in some way." I didn't see it then. But today, I can see it more clearly. My study of communication, like many professors I interviewed, is connected to the experiences of my childhood, my distaste for the way my parents engaged in conflict, and my conviction that people can communicate more positively.

Guided by Curiosity

"Why don't people talk to each other kindly?"
"What did the good teachers do that the bad teachers didn't do?"
"How do you get beyond binaries?"

The participants in this study were all reflective and curious. Many were driven by questions rather than answers. Participants engaged in the process of reflection as a way of learning and as a way of discovering themselves. Questions also provided a lifelong journey of learning: questions may never be fully answered, but they could guide the process of thinking, of learning, and of discovery.

Very often, the participants in the study revealed the questions that drove their thinking, particularly their research. The exploration of ideas and seeking answers to questions is at the heart of being a professor. Often, the scholars devoted their entire career to a single question that would only be partially answered. Steven Beebe's major question, for example, was "How do we communicate more effectively?" This question guided his research, his teaching, and his writing. It also became the question that guided his work as an administrator, especially in his role as chair of a department. "I'm very interested in the 'so what' question." He told me, "How does this [theory] help us communicate better? That's what I'm interested in. That's my big question."

Sometimes, as is the case with Karen Foss, the process of asking questions led to a fundamental change in the self. Karen said, "I realized I was a feminist bully and I needed to stop doing that." She laughed for a second, so I probed. "Well, tell me more about that," I asked. She replied with honesty:

> Well it relates to both everyday things and how I relate to people in the field. I mean, I came into the field from the women's movement and I wanted things to be a particular way, you know. I wanted the world to change so it was better for women. I didn't want women to change their names when they got married. I didn't think, I think women should think more about having children than they often do. I wanted the Equal Rights Amendment passed and then I thought of, you know, as part of this question of persuasion, I thought, well, *How are you any different?* You know you have this cause that you are trying to cram down people's throats and what difference does it make to you whether they become feminist or not? Or whether they change their names? So just stop it Foss!" (Laughs) "Let them live their lives like you want to be able to live your life."

What a powerful question to ask one's self: "How are you any different?" For Karen Foss, it was reflecting on that question and answering it truthfully that led to personal change. Both in teaching and everyday life, she worked at being more open to others' ways of thinking and to helping others discover their own thinking.

In his book on teaching, Ken Bain (2012) wrote: "You don't learn from experience. You learn from reflecting on experience" (p. 161). For scholars of communication, reflection was guided by an intense curiosity and a life-long question; a question complex enough that a person could only make progress towards an uncertain or tentative answer. The question would be a guiding framework for one's lifework.

Like Steven Beebe, John Daly's lifelong quest was to help people communicate better. At one point in the interview, he explained, "I really want people to be better communicators! That's my big one, I want people to be more effective when they communicate, more happy when they communicate, and I'm really into helping those people who don't know how, just get a little bit better." At this point in the interview, it was not yet framed as a guiding question, but the question appeared just a bit later: "I've always been deeply involved in how you teach people how to communicate more effectively. That would be my core thing, 'how do you make people more effective communicators?' Reflecting on that question guided John and Steven's careers.

For some professors, the guiding question more closely aligned with teaching. This was well captured in my interview with Gerry Philipsen, professor at the University of Washington and award-winning scholar and teacher, who cared about students and their learning. His focus, in fact, was not on teaching, per se, but on learning. Consider his lifelong question:

> Almost every day I think back to what happened to me as a student in these class-rooms, or in these activities and what made it possible for me to learn something. I just think about that all the time, how can somebody learn something? Something that is of intrinsic value, that is of some value to them in their lives?

What a big question to ponder: "How can somebody learn something?" With this question, Gerry could dedicate himself to seeking more profound answers. Perhaps this is why Raymie McKerrow, Charles E. Zumkehr Professor of Communication at Ohio University, pointed out in my interview with him: "I think the one constant is…I am still reading, I am still thinking."

The scholars I spoke to were very reflective. They reflected about teaching, they reflected about students' needs, they reflected about their research, and what they read. They reflected early on in their lives, as Allan Ward explained when he said, "I began to wonder as a child, Why do my parents believe these things about other groups?" But the reflection process was often guided by big questions. Questions that provided a framework to direct one's thinking, and ultimately fueled the love and passion that the scholars had for the discipline.

Passionate

One spring morning in Iowa, I walked to one of my favorite classes with Mr. Jensen. The class was Advanced Interpersonal Communication. By the time we reached the classroom he had already written a quotation on the board. On that day, he wrote the words of Søren Kierkegaard, that I have held onto since 1997. I walked in, sat down, opened my notebook, and wrote Kierkegaard's words of wisdom: "Passion is the measure of all things."

All of the participants in this study loved the field of communication. They loved to *think* about it. They loved to teach it. They loved to promote the discipline. And, they supported their love by the fact that they had dedicated their career to the field.

Their passion for the discipline was sometimes expressed in direct terms, but it was also cued by the way they talked about the discipline. Karen Foss said, "There is nothing more powerful than communication. It makes our realities...you can change a reality by changing a term." Sandra Petronio, professor at Indiana University, who created Communication Boundary Management Theory, explained, "what I like a lot about the discipline of communication is the fact that it permeates everything." Dan O'Hair echoed this point when he shared: "I am a true believer in the study of communication. There is nothing more exciting as a profession than the study of messages and audiences and media." Jon Nussbaum, Distinguished Honors Faculty at Penn State University, summed it up well, "I just think that it's amazing that we are in this amazing discipline. If we just keep our eyes open and we see all of this communication around us and that's really what our hypothesis comes from." The scholars expressed their love for the field of communication by their common belief in its significance.

For many, in fact, it was the impact that communication could have on the lives of others, and the inherent beauty of small moments, that triggered their passion. Sandra Petronio, for example, shared this experience:

> As we travel throughout our lifespan we start to notice different kinds of things about communication. When my daughter was little, it was fascinating to me to see how she learned how to talk and how she learned how to express herself and that made me think a lot about the communicative process but in the contexts of families and

especially with little kids. As she grew up, each stage had a different learning curve for me in terms of what communication really is, and that continues to be true. My daughter is all grown up and now a fully fledged adult. So I had to change how I communicated with her again as a fully fledged adult, because talking to her like she was 14 just wasn't working for us [laughs] … . I was divorced and re-married and each personal thing changed the way I thought about the impact of communication and it affected my teaching and the research that I did and the students I've had.

The applied nature of studying communication gave rise to passionate statements about the possible implications. Dawn O. Braithwaite explained the constitutive nature of communication. She said that communication is "the center point of who people are, how they become who they are, and what their experiences are…[it is] one of the most important things that we can teach people." For many scholars, communication could be applied to solve real problems—it was an energy that could be used to improve society. In his interview, Gary Kreps emphasized this point:

So I become very excited and enthusiastic about the applications of communication in society. And I have a lot of passion for trying to use communication to promote social justice and to use it as a way of empowering at-risk and stigmatized populations. And so, based on my experience working in these different areas, I recognize that communication has an even bigger potential than most people in our field recognize. It is not just a topic for education, it is also a really important topic for trying to address important social issues. So that is really helpful. And also I found that there are tremendous applications and I try to get my students excited about that. I really try to emphasize to them into realizing that the work you do in communication is not just getting credits in class, but helping them to address important issues and to do important things and to solve problems and to help people. So I am like a missionary. …I live with enthusiasm—which can be very infectious.

Communication is both an object of study and something we engage in every day. Being able to reflect on communication as a practice and to be confronted with its complexities and beauty fascinated many professors. The implications were both distant and personal. Arvind Singhal, for example, explained to me, "What I love about the field now is how intimately I and others whom I interact with are engaged in the practice of communication." This focus on everyday moments enabled Arvind to reflect about the change he could create with small actions:

Whether it is trying to convince your family to join you and you say that one message, "how am I going to frame it?" "Is it going to be interrogative?" "Or is it going to be a command?" "What carrots am I dangling now?" and making it comfortable for them. So it is an absolute, it's the glue. Which, if we are social animals, it's the glue which allows the things to happen and the outcomes of how things happen good or bad because there will be outcomes that are fairly dependent on what the form and what the content of these messages are. And so that is what fascinates me about this discipline that while I can be working with Soap Operas, designing them so that they create certain types of conversations about issues that people haven't had. At the same time, in my personal day-to-day life it allows me to see the beauty—that discipline has manifest into practice.

Communication professors believe in the power of communication—in its constitutive nature, its consequences, and the possibilities for social change. Perhaps, the passion that many scholars feel about their object of study was best expressed in the hopes and dreams of Allan Ward, who shared with me the transformative force of communicating better. The field of communication, he said, "can transform individuals and relationships between individuals." "Far beyond learning a discipline," he added, "it can be transformative for individuals, for groups, and hence for society." Consider these final words:

Every step that is taken, no matter how small it seems, toward that change is a ripple effect that can go on. Every student we affect will work differently with his or her family with their children and they'll be better off. The children will be better off and their children. The impact that we can have toward peace and communication and understanding and cooperation are among those things.

The communication professors I spoke to were indeed passionate about their field of study. For them, and to echo the words of Kierkegaard, the field of communication was "the measure of all things." It was expressed in their words, and in a palpable energy throughout my conversations. It was both in the content of what was said and in how it was expressed. To share a last example, then, Betsy Bach, professor at the University of Montana and past president of the National Communication Association, shared the story of a friend who questioned the value of studying communication. Consider the way she defended the discipline:

I was talking to a friend, who is a relatively arrogant pulmonologist, not too long ago, and he goes, "Oh why do you study communication? I mean for God's sake, we all communicate!" I am like, "Bill, I don't need to tell you about pulmonology, it is just breathing, right?"

Conclusion

This chapter described commonalities across participants in this study. Specifically, I found that communication professors tend to have some affinity with communication. Many professors began in debate, enjoyed public speaking, or appreciated the written word. In studying the discipline, many found an alignment between who they were, their strengths, if you will, and the disciplinary content. Second, many communication professionals are sensitive to human interaction. It is also probably accurate that people around them are tone-deaf, unable to see and hear what they can see and hear. Nevertheless, across the interviews, I found that many communication professionals were already attuned with, and observant of, human interaction—more so than the average person. In fact, and related, many communication professors' early life experiences guided them toward this field of study and cultivated the strengths, abilities, and questions that would guide their professional lives. Finally, the communication professional is reflective, guided by a core question, and passionate about the object of study.

It is true that passion is the real measure of all things. What else could drive a person to study something for their entire professional career? But passion is not enough. The fire can die quickly. There are too many challenges, life experiences, and obstacles in the course of a career. Perhaps, then, passion leads to love—a more tranquil, more powerful and lasting force. In the final chapter of his book, *Speaking Into the Air*, John Peters (1999) reflected on the power of communication—what it is and what it could be—its possibilities and limitations. In one paragraph, there is a sentence that exemplifies the nature of the communication professors I interviewed. Peters wrote: "No profession of love is as convincing as a lifetime of fidelity" (p. 271). All of our participants expressed their love for the field, but the difference between me and them is that they were still engaged in it. They had dedicated themselves to teaching, research, and service over the course of their entire professional lives and had expressed through deed rather than words a "lifetime of fidelity."

References

Bain, K. (2004). *What the best college teachers do.* Cambridge, MA: Harvard University Press.

Bain, K. (2012). *What the best college students do.* Cambridge, MA: Harvard University Press.

Boyer, E. L. (1990). *Scholarship reconsidered: Priorities of the professoriate.* Princeton, NJ: The Carnegie Foundation for the Advancement of Teaching.

Craig, R. T. (1999). Communication theory as a field. *Communication Theory, 9*(2), 119–161.

Gardner, H. (2006). *Five minds for the future.* Harvard Business Press.

Haynes, A. (2010). *Writing successful academic books.* Cambridge, England: Cambridge University Press.

Lindlof, T. R., & Taylor, B. C. (2011). *Qualitative communication research methods.* Thousand Oaks, CA: Sage.

McKeachie, W., & Svinicki, M. (2014). *McKeachie's teaching tips.* Belmont, CA: Wadsworth.

Palmer, P. J. (2007). *The courage to teach: Exploring the inner landscape of a teacher's life.* New York, NY: Wiley & Sons.

Peters, J. D. (1999). *Speaking into the air: A history of the idea of communication.* Chicago, IL: The University of Chicago Press.

Rogers, E. (1994). *A history of communication study: A biographical approach.* New York, NY: The Free Press.

Van de Ven, A. H. (2007). *Engaged scholarship: A guide for organizational and social research.* Oxford, England; New York, NY: Oxford University Press.

Weber, R., & Fuller, R. (2012). *Statistical methods for communication researchers and professionals.* Dubuque, IA: Kendal Hunt.

Wulff, D. H., & Austin, A. E. (2004). *Paths to the professoriate: Strategies for enriching the preparation of future faculty.* San Francisco, CA: Jossey-Bass.

· 3 ·
HOW DO COMMUNICATION PROFESSORS GROW?

My student Sayra comes into my office. She has been working diligently on a project for 9 months. In a couple weeks, she will deliver a 25-minute presentation in front of faculty, alumni, and friends of the department. Capstone Day, as we call it, is a unique experience for students. In the fall, all seniors write a 25-page research paper. In the spring, they must present it effectively. If they do not meet the time frame, they fail the presentation and therefore do not graduate. This is a pressure-packed day, but Sayra wrote a beautiful research paper and has been practicing day in and day out. In her last practice, I had nothing left to recommend. It was simply excellent. Yet, she comes into my office, bursting with anxious energy. "What if I fail?" "I can't take it," "I still have so much to do," her voice cracks. I ask her to sit with me, but she says "no" at first. As we talk a little more, the negative energy dissipates. I invite her to sit again. I want to make my message clear. "Sayra," I say with all seriousness and a direct gaze,

you've worked hard, you have excelled in every practice, this is the moment you've been waiting for. You are graduating and you will succeed. Now is not the time to doubt yourself. Instead, enjoy every moment of your success. You have earned the right to ride the wave now. There is no need to struggle. You're on top of the board and all you have to do is let the water guide you.

I slow down my speech purposefully: "Ride … the … wave."

Of course, I would love for Sayra to learn to ride the wave in this one moment, to see it now and to experience it as a turning point. But this study shows that personal growth is not accomplished in a singular moment. It is, to draw on the words of Lynn Turner, professor of Communication at Marquette University, "*a gradual awakening*," a slow process that unfolds over the lifespan.

This chapter describes how communication professors personally grew and developed. I show that throughout their lifespan, communication professionals slowly and gradually moved in more productive directions. This development, to quote Arvind Singhal, is "more evolutionary than revolutionary." To support this proposal, the chapter draws first on the work of Carl Rogers, the famous third-force psychologist, to give context to the notion of personal growth. Then, I show how communication scholars "gradually awoke" toward self-confidence and ultimately toward others.

The Process of Becoming a Person

One of my favorite articles is an ethnographic report on Olympic swimmers titled "The Mundanity of Excellence." In that article, Dan Chambliss (1988) argued that moving toward excellence is not achieved by making quantitative changes in one's conduct or practice, but is instead achieved by making *qualitative* changes. Quantitative improvements, he explained, "involve doing *more of the same thing*." Qualitative improvements, in contrast, "involve doing *different kinds of things*." According to his study, swimmers do not move up a ladder of excellence, but instead move from one social world to another. In those social worlds, swimmers do things qualitatively differently, with the best doing things very differently than beginners.

His work suggests three dimensions that are points of qualitative difference in swimmers across those social worlds. The first one is technique. At different levels of performance, practitioners swim in distinctive technical terms. "The styles of strokes, dives, and turns," Chambliss (1988) wrote, "are dramatically different at different levels" (p. 73). The second dimension is discipline. "The best swimmers," he wrote, "are more likely to be strict with their training, coming to workouts on time, carefully doing the competitive strokes legally, watch what they eat, sleep regular hours, do proper warm-ups before a meet, and the like" (p. 73). Third is attitude. At the highest levels of the sport, "there is an inversion of attitude" (p. 74). What swimmers may find boring early in their careers, they now love or strive on. For example, many beginners find swimming back and forth for several hours boring or difficult. At the highest level, it is seen as a moment of personal meditation. To put it simply, then, the growth of an Olympic swimmer is not achieved by making quantitative adjustments, but by making qualitative ones.

Chambliss's (1988) study of excellence offers a point of reflection to understand human development over the lifetime. Participants in this study revealed that they changed *qualitatively* in their ways of thinking, in their self-perception, and in the ways that they approach others. The difference between who they were early in their careers and who they are now was not based on numbers; it was captured by qualitative differences in how they saw themselves and in their attitudes toward others.

Seeking excellence in an art or practice is one way to understand human development. Another is to consider scholarship on self-actualization. One such example is the work of the famous third-force psychologist Carl Rogers, whose writing has influenced communication theory and practice across contexts (for example, see Anderson, Baxter, & Cissna, 2003; Cissna & Anderson, 2012). In his book *On Becoming a Person*, Carl Rogers (1961) described what happens to individuals as they move toward becoming "a fully-functional human being," a phrase that is similar to Maslow's concept of self-actualization. He wrote, "it seems to me that at bottom each person is asking, 'who am I really? How can I get in touch with this real self, underlying all my surface behavior? How can I become myself?'" (p. 108).

Based on his observations and experience with client-centered therapy, Rogers (1961) proposed that individuals could answer these lifelong questions by taking more productive directions. He argued that the process of becoming a fully functional person may involve moving *away* from certain tendencies and moving *toward* certain ways of being (see Table 1). Viewed from his perspective, self-actualization is not a state of being, but instead "a continuing way of life" (p. 181) and a process of living, learning, and becoming.

Table 1. Becoming a Person

Moving Away From ...	Moving Toward ...
... façade	... self-direction
... oughts	... being a process
... meeting other people's expectations	... being complexity
... pleasing others	... open to experience
... external evaluation	... trust of self

As seen in Table 1, individuals move away from certain ways of thinking and being. First, Rogers (1961) observed that his clients moved away from façades. He wrote, "the client shows a tendency to move away, hesitantly and fearfully, from a self that he is *not*" (p. 167). In order words, there is less and less pretending and more and more acceptance about being one's self. Second, as people grow more productively, they move away from living up to obligations that are not their own; they move away from "oughts." As Rogers explained, "some individuals have absorbed so deeply from their parents the concept 'I ought to be good,' or 'I have to be good,'" that it is only with the greatest of inward struggle that they find themselves moving away from this goal" (p. 168). In addition, they move away from seeking to meet other people's expectations or to please others. Finally, they move away from acting with an external locus of evaluation and begin to live for themselves. Self-actualizing individuals, then, move away from choosing "anything which is artificial, anything which is imposed, anything which is defined from without" (p. 170).

As people move away from certain tendencies, they simultaneously take on new directions. First, they move toward self-direction. They increasingly take responsibility for themselves and become more autonomous. Second, they move "toward being a process" (Rogers, 1961, p. 171). They see themselves as being "in flux," developing, learning, and growing; they are engaged in a process of self-discovery. Third, they increasingly appreciate the complexity of being human. Every person, they begin to see, is full of contradictory emotions, stances, attitudes, and beliefs. Fourth, and as a result, they become more open to experience. The individual, Rogers (1961) explained, "moves toward living in an open, friendly, close relationship to his own experience" (p. 173). Finally, they trust their thoughts, their ideas, and their creativity more and more.

In short, as people move away from certain tendencies and toward certain directions, each person "is coming closer to being himself" (Rogers, 1961, p. 167). Carl Rogers' proposal about healthy human development is remarkably similar to the ways in which communication professionals talked about their own development. They increasingly trusted their impulses, felt less fearful about trying new things, and saw themselves as life-long learners. Specifically, though, we found two dominant themes. Our participants gradually awakened toward self-confidence and moved in the direction of others. The rest of the chapter provides evidence for these two directions.

Gradual Awakening Toward Self-Confidence

In my interview with Wendy Leeds-Hurwitz, who is currently involved in a project that will trace the intellectual genealogies of our discipline, she drew on a conversation with a friend, who shared with her his experience doing interviews with professors. She said, "he got the best interviews from full professors." "Assistant professors," she reported, "were too insecure, associate professors were too inappropriately full of themselves, and it was the full professors who were secure and willing to make the time to talk to him." Although this is a generalization from a developmental perspective, the participants in this study consistently reported gaining more and more confidence as their careers advanced. They slowly moved toward trusting themselves, accepting their strengths and weaknesses, and growing in the direction of self-confidence. They were gradually awakening to themselves. The overall process was well captured by Betsy Bach when she explained (using the third person) what happened to her throughout her career:

> I think, you know, Betsy before she learned about communication, and that may be as much my personality as it is my communication, but in some level the two are inevitably linked, you know. Betsy was kind of shy, kind of quiet, kind of unsure if her opinions would be taken seriously and even afraid to offer an opinion. Now, Betsy knows, you know, a lot about communication and I am unafraid to share my thoughts and opinion, but because I study communication, I now know how to share my thoughts, opinion, ideas in a way that isn't overbearing, isn't narcissistic, like "Oh lady, shut up, you are not the expert on everything."

One of the ways that the participants cued this development was in the way that they approached the classroom. They gained confidence in how to proceed and a sense of trust and faith in the process, and in themselves. As Carl Rogers (1961) explained, the fully functional person is "increasing trust in his organism" (p. 189); "they discover to an ever-increasing degree that if they are open to their experience, doing what 'feels right' proves to be a competent and trustworthy guide to behavior" (p. 189). In my interview with Arvind Singhal, a thought leader who is affecting practice across the globe, he described his experience in the classroom as trusting the process. He said, "I trust the process. If the university trusts me to teach a class of course I'll have a syllabus, but sometimes I tend to first be developing the syllabus with the students." He added:

I don't have to worry and I have a sense of what it is they are reading. I enter the classroom with really no plan and I've become good at it and I know I've become good at it because I am now increasingly mindful every second of the classroom. And there are some principles which will allow me to because I know I can begin a class with, what did you read? And what stands out? And that comfort is there now to trust the process. So it has become a patterned habit in that sense and I don't do too much advance prep for anything in all the interaction we have where, you know, let's begin where we are at and let's see where we go and we will end up at a different place where we didn't know we would end up, but would be different if I had a canned presentation.

Arvind's ability to trust the process and to teach "in the moment" exemplifies how individuals in the study increasingly approached the classroom and their lives. It was embodied by trusting themselves, their actions, and having faith that the process would unfold productively.

Drawing on Carl Rogers, another way that individuals could awake their confidence was by increasingly being open to new experiences. In my interview with Gary Kreps, who, among other projects, served at the Founding Chief of Health Communication and Informatics Research at the National Cancer Institute, he discussed how he expanded his view of the applications of his scholarship. This is what he shared:

> Well I think it gave me more confidence to work with different audiences in different places. It also encouraged me to pursue different kinds of applications and not to be limited in scope. I think that some people think of doing their work in one realm, but as I continued to grow, I started to realize that my work fits into many different realms, many different walks of life, many different types of organizations, many different countries, so I have a pretty broad frame now and I have the confidence to work in those different realms.

Of note in this moment is when he said: "As I continue to grow." These words are important because they capture well what it was like for most participants: a process of becoming, not a state of being. Said differently, participants did not move from being without confidence to being confident. Instead, they moved in the direction of increasing confidence. This way of thinking was pointed out by Carl Rogers (1961) in his work. "The good life," he wrote, "is not any fixed state. It is not in my estimation, a state of virtue, or contentment, or nirvana, or happiness. It is not a condition in which the individual is adjusted, or fulfilled, or actualized" (p. 186). Instead, "the good life is a process" (p. 186). Participants, thus, were *slowly gaining* confidence.

One of the most acute descriptions of this process occurred in my con-versation with my colleague Carol Thompson, professor at the University of Arkansas at Little Rock and winner of the most prestigious teaching award on campus. Consider how she described her development and growth throughout her lifespan.

> If you look at say the last 30 years day by day you don't think any change is hap-pening, but when you look at it in retrospect and I look back 30 years I go "oh wow something happened here." Early on, I was an incredibly shy individual and I had difficulty in interpersonal relationships and I liked public speaking because I could prepare for that...so that's your starting place, feeling incompetent, and then you move by degrees and you have experiences along the way, hurts and mysteries that you have to solve with people and experiences you have...all of these things melt together....I can say this having been one, is very self-involved because you're kind of concerned with how everyone is going to see you, how everyone will think of you.... I shouldn't do that and then they are going to think badly of me you know, but as you move on and you get more confident and you get more assured then you can begin to focus your attention because you're no longer focused on [your]self so much. You start focusing on other people and so when I hit that other milestone and I don't know exactly what it was, but when I hit that milestone the focus shifted from me and how people received me to what's happening to you. I put this in practice and I begin to see you as a real human being.

Many scholars gradually awakened to self-confidence. But as they gained con-fidence, their perspective, their ways of seeing, and their focus all became different. More and more, the participants described, they gradually awakened to others.

Gradual Awakening Toward Others

My conversation with Carol Thompson further revealed the natural shift that took place over the lifespan from focusing on the self to focusing on others. Interview after interview, participants expressed this slow, and gradual, awak-ening to others. There was a distinct shift that took place in professors' think-ing, in their approach to the world, in the way to teach in the classroom, and in their way of being. Carol said, "it's a combination of self-development as a human being." She slowed down her speech, used her hands to communicate, and expressed it firmly. "It is getting to a point of maturity where you don't have to be center stage," she said. "I was fulfilling something within myself that I lacked. I needed to shine. I needed to be. I needed to have some value because I didn't think I had much value, and so at that point of maturity finally figuring out that I am." She echoed the message that as confidence grew, there was less a need to prove yourself to others, or to meet their expectations. But in the end of this discussion, she expressed the movement toward others. She affirmed the message:

> You don't need [the glory] and so you come out of that saying, "what is important?" And what is important is establishing those relationships and focusing in on the thou or the human being of that person and trying to figure out that the person is very much the one that I am and to me that's the progression.

When Carol spoke of the "thou," she was drawing on the philosopher Martin Buber. In his work, Buber (1958) argued that people often treat each other as objects or instruments to reach personal gain. He called this way of relating an I-it relationship. In contrast, he called each person to engage with others in an I-thou relationship. This is created by respecting the other deeply, confirming their experience, and by being personally authentic and genuine. Carol's last line is critical, then, because it reflects a new way of being with others and a movement away from self-interest and toward meeting another wholeheartedly.

John Peters, who wrote about how the idea of communication evolved through time, expressed this same point. I asked him about how his understanding of communication had shifted through time. He said, there is "an inherent gap between the kind of egotistical vision we have of ourselves and who we really are, and how we are really coming across." "In communication," he added, "we are always ourselves, but we're also always others. That to me is the key lesson." He paused to mark his point: "The self is the other, the other is the self."

John Peters' point is complex (see Peters, 1999). On the one hand, it suggests that persons in conversations are not willing to see themselves for who they really are. In communication, this creates friction and the impossibility of meeting one other authentically. Each person's self-perceptions, and the perceptions of the other, may be inaccurate or exaggerated. On the other hand, his comment also implies that people are more similar than they are different and that human interaction could be approached with this perspective. So his comment is also affirming. "If you can recognize the self in the other," John told me again, "and recognize the other in the self, then you've figured out how communication works." To have this realization, I would say, one must look beyond the self and see the other first. The person must move from looking inward to looking outward—which is exactly what Carol Thompson was expressing: a movement away from the self and toward seeing the other.

The movement toward others was expressed by communication scholars in a variety of ways. Some framed this development in light of their thinking about communication. Steven Beebe, who co-authored many textbooks on public speaking, small group, and interpersonal communication (e.g., Beebe, Beebe, & Ivy, 2015), for example, said, "it gets back to being other oriented, audience-centered, needs-centered." "It's not about you," he told me, "it's about the other person." "So in communication," he shared with me, "it's always about adapting to the listener …it's about the other person." Em Griffin, whose books include *Making Friends* (1987), *Getting Together* (1982), and *The Mind Changers* (1976), expressed a similar perspective but grounded it in practice even more. You have to "work real hard to find out and consider, what does this person need? What are their needs and desires?" He added, "and if you consider that, you can adjust your communication to try and have their needs and desires met. And quite possibly there might be some overlap between your needs and desires, but it's an other-centered approach."

Many scholars talked about being other-centered, but the point I am making here, is that other-centeredness is not a state of being, but *a process of becoming*. For example, Gary Kreps, author of more than 50 books and edited volumes on health communication, said, "I try to be sensitive to others' issues and concerns. I listen to them as much as I can. I think maybe in the past I was more self-centered." The word "more" is a good cue here—participants were less self-centered, but it was not completely absent. The shift toward others was a direction, not a destination. This is well illustrated in comments made by Gerry Philipsen, recipient of the Distinguished Scholar Award from the National Communication Association:

> I think I have become more attentive to building up the other person and validating them and supporting them. I think there was a time when I was so concerned with the hearing of me than other people. I was concerned with that. More concerned with myself than I was concerned with myself as an instrument that could be supportive to other people.

The movement is in the direction of others. With increasing confidence and trust, participants in this study reported increasingly moving in the direction of others. Carol Thompson called it "decentering." She said,

There is a division, there is something that happens as you mature, which allows you or at least allowed me to have another focus. I think it is the process of decentering, stepping outside of oneself, and attempting to reach someone else's center.

The gaze moves from inward to outward, from understanding the self to understanding others.

Conclusion

The communication professors we interviewed revealed two simultaneous *qualitative* tendencies in the way they developed through time. On the one hand, the participants reported increasingly gaining confidence, trust in themselves, and having faith in the process. On the other hand, they reported a movement toward others. To quote Lynn Turner again, communication scholars' development was a gradual awakening. They moved toward confidence and other people, and away from fear and examining the self. They moved toward self-acceptance and the affirmation of others. This development is remarkably similar to what Carl Rogers (1961) described in the fully functional person.

In his ethnography of swimmers, Chambliss (1988) noted that professionals achieve excellence by progressing in three realms: (1) the techniques that they use, (2) the discipline that they have, and (3) the attitude they take toward their art or themselves. This chapter described the latter—how communication professors' personal attitudes changed through time. The major finding is that communication scholars progress toward self-acceptance and an interest in the other. This is important for anyone interested in communicating more effectively. Simply communicating more often will not improve interaction (see research on expertise by Ericsson & Pool, 2016). It is making a qualitative change in one's approach to interaction that will make the difference. From the perspective of our participants, those qualitative differences include gaining personal congruence and de-centering, becoming authentic, and developing empathy. These are not states of being, but should instead be viewed as directions of personal growth and development. In later chapters, we will explore the technical aspects of communicating well and the discipline it takes to enact them. In the meantime, this chapter underscores that excellence in the art of communication is achieved by affirming both our self and the other.

Like my student Sayra, I wish I too could ride the wave and have the confidence of a lifetime, but the truth is that I am slowly working on it. And I need the help of others. This became evident a few weeks ago when I was having a tough week. At the time, I served as interim chair for another department, working with faculty and students from a different discipline. The context was difficult. At night, I would discuss this with my wife, expressing my stress, my fears, and my struggles. One morning, I came to the office and turned my computer on as I always do, ready to write. I opened my e-mail to make sure there was no emergency. There was one e-mail from my wife, which surprised me, first because we rarely e-mail each other, and second because the subject line of the e-mail said: "Ride the Wave." I double clicked on the e-mail to open it and found a picture of a surfer inside a wave with my photograph edited over his face. It's me riding a wave. Right underneath, my wife wrote: "Ride the wave baby. Ride the wave."

References

Anderson, R., Baxter, L. A., & Cissna, K. N. (Eds.). (2003). *Dialogue: Theorizing difference in communication studies*. Thousand Oaks, CA: Sage.

Beebe, S. A., Beebe, S. J., & Ivy, D. K. (2015). *Communication principles for a lifetime* (6th Ed.). NY: Pearson.

Buber, M. (1958). The I-thou theme, contemporary psychotherapy, and psychodrama. *Pastoral Psychology*, 9(5), 57–58.

Chambliss, D. F. (1988). The mundanity of excellence: An ethnographic report on stratification and Olympic swimmers. *Sociological Theory*, 7(1), 70–86.

Cissna, K. N., & Anderson, R. (2012). *Moments of meeting: Buber, Rogers, and the potential for public dialogue*. Albany, NY: State University of New York Press.

Ericsson, A., & Pool, R. (2016). *Peak: Secrets from the new science of expertise*. New York: Houghton Mifflin Harcourt.

Griffin, E. (1976). *The mind changers: The art of Christian persuasion*. Carol Stream, IL: Tyndale House.

Griffin, E. (1982). *Getting together: A guide for good groups*. Madison, WI: InterVarsity Press.

Griffin, E. (1987). *Making friends (& making them count)*. Madison, WI: InterVarsity Press.

Peters, J. D. (1999). *Speaking into the air: A history of the idea of communication*. Chicago, IL: The University of Chicago Press.

Rogers, C. (1961). *On becoming a person*. Boston, MA: Houghton Mifflin.

· 4 ·

HOW DO COMMUNICATION
PROFESSORS VIEW TEACHING?

"One of my philosophies of teaching," Steven Beebe told me, is "it's better to get a message out of someone than it is to put one in them." All of the participants in the study are or were actively teaching throughout their careers. There is, in fact, in each of them a strong desire to reach students, to help them, to support them, and to foster learning. The communication professors we interviewed loved students, loved to see them learn and grow, and through time became more and more student-centered teachers. This chapter unpacks this development in light of recent research on teaching excellence. It describes what the best teachers do and then highlights that teaching excellence is a process rather than a state of being. The chapter answers these questions: How did they develop as teachers? What did they move from and to? And what changes have taken place? The answer to these questions lies in what we often attribute to the best teachers.

The Nature of Teaching Excellence

In his study of the best college teachers, Ken Bain (2004) collected data from 63 different teachers who were nationally selected for their teaching effectiveness. Together with his team, he conducted in-depth formal and informal interviews, collected syllabi and assignments, observed classroom interaction, analyzed students' products, and interviewed colleagues who were familiar with their teaching. What emerged from analyzing these data are the characteristics of teaching excellence, which are described in his book, *What the Best College Teachers Do*.

First, Bain (2004) found that outstanding teachers think about teaching primarily in light of *learning*. For most participants in the study, teaching was not about "transmitting knowledge and building a storehouse of information in the students' brains" (p. 16). Instead, the best teachers think about teaching as "helping learners grapple with ideas and information to construct understanding" (p. 6). The best teachers do not transmit information, they co-construct knowledge with students.

Second, the best teachers prepare carefully: they focus not on what *they* should do in the classroom, but rather on what *students* should do. Instead of asking, "What should I teach?" they ask: "What should my students learn and how can I facilitate that learning?" By flipping the question, the best teachers change the script of classroom interaction.

Third, the best teachers, Bain (2004) also found, have high expectations for students. They believe that if students engage in the process, they will naturally be successful. They trust that students will rise to the challenges that are placed in front of them and they have faith in students' potential to learn. Outstanding teachers, Bain wrote, "look for and appreciate the individual value of each student" (p. 72).

Fourth, the best college professors use different approaches; some lecture, some lead action-based exercises, and some adhere to the Socratic Method. But they all have one thing in common. They foster "a natural critical learning environment" (p. 18). Students, Bain (2004) explained, "learn by confronting intriguing, beautiful, or important problems, authentic tasks that will challenge them to grapple with ideas, rethink assumptions, and examine their mental models of reality" (p. 18). The best teachers create a safe space to learn, to think critically, and to ask more questions.

Fifth, great faculty consistently assess their efforts to see if learning is really occurring. The purpose of assessment is not to evaluate students' performance, but to see where each student is on the journey of learning. As Bain (2004) put it, the outstanding teachers use "assessment to help students learn, not just to rate and rank their efforts" (p. 151). In other words, they assess students' learning to help them learn even more.

Overall, then, Ken Bain (2004) found that the best college professors are student-focused and learning-focused (also see Weimer, 2002). They do whatever is necessary to create deep learning for students rather than surface learning, two concepts that emerged from empirical research by Marton and Säljö (1976). In their work, Biggs and Tang (2007) describe deep learning and surface learning as intentions and approaches to learning that students take. When engaging in surface learning, students focus on memorizing facts, seek to find the right answer, and accumulate information with the purpose of getting it right. Students who engage in deep learning, however, focus on the process, not the outcome. They approach learning with an intrinsic curiosity, connect ideas in readings or in the field, dig beneath the surface to understand the concept or theory, and seek to apply it to their own lives. Students who engage in deep learning obviously gain more from their experiences and perform at a higher level. Ultimately, students choose how they want to learn: to approach the task meaningfully and deeply or to do what is necessary to pass an examination.

What Ken Bain (2004) noticed in his study is that the best college teachers fostered deep learning, not surface learning. Of course, learning begins with the student's attitude and approach, but teachers can create an environment in which students engage in learning more deeply. Teachers who cultivate a deep approach to learning tend to have passion and personal interest in the subject. They concentrate on what matters most—they are not concerned about covering content. They focus on confronting students' misconceptions about the discipline. They engage students in active learning. They assess students' learning to see if they are getting it (see Biggs & Tang, 2007). The best teachers ask themselves: "What kind of intellectual and personal development do I want my students to enjoy in this class, and what evidence might I collect about the nature and progress of their development?" (Bain, 2004, p. 152). They focus on intended learning outcomes and promote a learning-based approach: students are not asked to perform, but to learn. Finally, in a deep learning approach, students are encouraged to make mistakes and to fail without penalty. The best teachers, then, encourage deep learning and invite students to take a chance on a journey of personal growth.

In light of research on teaching excellence, this study reveals our communication professors' approach to teaching and how they grew as teachers. I describe their realizations and their turning points. Teaching excellence, I argue, is not a destination. It is a life-long process. Ken Bain's (2004) book is remarkable in describing how the best teachers approach the classroom, but it also implies that teaching excellence is a state of being. What this study shows is that across all teachers, there was a movement toward excellence, a movement toward learner-centered teaching, and toward deep learning. The participants in this study *became* better teachers through time. Specifically, the interviews revealed consistent directions in the approach to teaching of communication professors. They moved *toward* (a) students and their learning, (b) listening rather than speaking, and, ultimately (c), creating experiential learning for students. In short, they became learner-centered teachers (Weimer, 2002).

A Movement Toward Students and Their Learning

Kristine Muñoz is professor at the University of Iowa, but her journey started as an undergraduate student in Texas and continued as a graduate student at the University of Washington, where she met Gerry Philipsen. In her interview, she described the experience of learning from Gerry as a turning point: "Gerry was much more of a 'pick one spot and go down very deeply' and not once but every quarter go down very deeply and keep on going down very deeply into the same spot." What she experienced in that course was what researchers call deep learning—a preferred mode of learning that leaves long-lasting impact. But her learning experience in the classroom was shaped by a lifelong question that Gerry spoke about in my interview with him: "How can somebody learn something?" "I think about it every day."

Across the board, the professors I interviewed loved learning, loved teaching, and through time focused more and more on students. John Peters exemplified this well when I asked him what he loved the most about the field. He said: "My students." Em Griffin shared: "The greatest satisfaction for me is still with students. Some of my best friends are former students." Myria Allen, who earned her doctorate from the University of Kentucky and later joined the faculty at the University of Arkansas at Fayetteville, spoke about an epiphany in the way that she approached the classroom:

> I had an epiphany probably about 10 years ago and I always found that going into the classroom incredibly challenging. If they don't like you it hurt emotionally, but at that epiphany, I went and did reflection on what I would rather do in my life besides teaching college students. And I thought absolutely nothing. That epiphany made the classroom more of a pleasure. Before I thought of myself more as a researcher. Now I saw myself as someone with a story to tell.

Myria Allen's epiphany was only 10 years ago; a small moment in the scheme of an entire career, but it fermented the process that many scholars experienced. They moved more and more toward student learning. Today, she explained, "I am at the stage where now I am most interested in mentoring young scholars." "It's time for me to help lift up young scholars and young students."

Myria's experience was similar to Karen Foss, who explained this lifespan development in her approach to teaching:

> When you are a teacher, you are more concerned with getting through the class period or having that material or imparting knowledge. Now I think I am much more interested in creating an environment in which people, my students, can explore the ideas that we are talking about in their own ways. So, I think I spend much more time on environment creation, I do not lecture as much, I kind of lay things out and let it go.

Karen Foss kept sharing.

> I guess, just simply not afraid of trying. I mean, now I just try new things. I trust that I'm going to pull this off, whatever that is without massive amounts of lecturing and preparation. So I guess I am just much more relaxed as a teacher.

This ability to relax in the classroom gave more space for students to learn. To quote Arvind Singhal, the communication professors we interviewed "trusted the process" more than ever. They wanted to see where learning could go, where interaction with students could move to. In a very real way, they embraced student learning by allowing it to occur. As an example, consider the way Valerie Manusov explained her development as a teacher:

> Back when I first started, I worked so hard. I put so many hours in to really prepare to be like I knew what I was talking about, or at least could seem like I knew what I was talking about. And so I would say I had a lot more energy back then but also a lot more insecurity about my own understanding. And now I would say I have less energy and I put less time into it but I have been teaching this so long and reflecting on this so long that for most topics I go into the classroom feeling very confident...when I was young I felt like I had to be in charge of everything, that I was sort of responsible for the whole discussion but over time I have realized that really I am responsible for helping to generate the discussion, but the more the students have to engage, again undergraduate or graduate, I see this particularly with graduate students, but the more I can find things that are engaging for them and then let them just go with it. I feel very comfortable, I do not worry about what direction it's going to go and I do not

worry about not making sure I have the things that I need to say because whatever it's going to come out, it is going to work for the students. So I think that the biggest difference is, I feel like I do not have to hold on so tight anymore.

Frank Lloyd Wright once asked a group of students to take their right hand and make a tight fist. Then, he asked them to slowly open their hand so that the palm would be facing up. After this gesture he said, "this is the whole story of learning" (Baker, 1977, p. 4). I agree with him, but perhaps, opening the hand is also the whole story of teaching. Early in their career, the communication professors entered the classroom with a tighter fist. Kristine Muñoz, for example, shared Valerie's experience. "When I first started up," she explained, "I was so terrified that I over prepared and had to control every minute of every class session." But, now, she added. "I can respond to students. I can let my students take the lead and I can relate, listen to them, and respond to them."

As the faculty slowly opened their hands, they became more flexible. They were much more interested in students and their learning. This development was well expressed by Michael Kleine. Michael is professor emeritus at the University of Arkansas at Little Rock where he started his career more than 30 years ago. As a person, he is gentle in his approach and humbling. As a teacher, his energy is focused on students. In the interview, he said:

> The biggest epiphany for me as a teacher was when I realized that I learned the most when I was in a teaching position, maybe more than the students. So as a result, I try and put my students in teaching positions as much as possible, so that way they are learning even more, and when they do that I become their student in a sense. So that move, at first I was threatened by it; I was like, "I'm not sure I am doing my job, etc.," but I found it to be a dynamic that is incredibly productive. My students tell me that they really like that and get a lot out of it so that was a huge change for me as a teacher, and realizing I could learn from my students.

The movement represented by Michael Kleine is a movement from teaching students to learning with or from students. It is a paradigm shift in one's approach to the classroom. The faculty in this study saw their own teaching journey as moving in that direction. Their role was not to teach, but to create what Ken Bain described as a critical learning environment—a safe space for students to play with ideas, to express themselves, and to confront the material. Raymie McKerrow, for example, expressed even more strongly what Michael Kleine shared. He told me, "If you aren't willing to learn from your own students, you should get out of the game." Raymie, who was drawn to academic work from his undergraduate experience in the classroom, believed that the whole focus should be students:

> I even tell undergraduates, you have ideas that can instruct me in ways I haven't thought about things. I am not the only person that has ideas here in the classroom. It is a little harder to work with undergraduates in that way, but if you open up that possibility for them and they believe that you are sincere, they will open up more and challenge themselves to express new ideas.

Focusing on students is not a cliché. The focus on students was made visible by the ways that participants talked about their experiences. In my interview with Lynn Turner, for instance, she often answered my questions in light of her work with students. Karen Foss also reflected a student-centered approach. In the interview, she mentioned reading the book *My Freshman Year*, written by an anthropology professor who enrolled in college again to understand her students (see Nathan, 2006). "So I read this book," Karen said, and "thought: 'Oh! I have to change my classes.'" Notice in the next part of her discourse, the way Karen's new approach to teaching was built around her empathy for her students and their needs:

> So I developed a self-paced system for teaching most of my classes, my undergraduate classes and public speaking, where they decide what grade they want. They therefore do the assignments necessary to get to that grade, they have to reach a certain level to move on to the next assignment, and they can come to class when they have something to do. But if they do not have something to do, whether it is to give a presentation or take a quiz or whatever, they do not have to come to class because, you know, especially at UNM, where students are working 40 hours a week, they have four children, they are 45 years old, they do not need a teacher who has this rigid attendance policy that is designed to do what? I don't know! If they do not want to be there, I don't need to have them there, you know? [Laughs]. So I think that has been a huge change that has made my classes much more fun, the students love it, it just works for everybody.

Interview after interview, the participants in the study expressed a movement toward students and their learning. In fact, meeting and interacting with students were at the heart of what gave meaning to the faculty's professional career. Toward the end of my interview with Karen Foss, she said, "let's try to support the students in figuring out who they are, who they are going to be, and help them get there. It does not have to be my path at all." Raymie McKerrow explained, "I am still in touch with two or three students from my 20 years in Maine. I am still in touch with several more students in my past 20 years here." "So," he added, "that is probably what I have done better than anything else. It is having an impact on students' lives in a positive way and that's what keeps me going." For John Daly, the joy was seeing students become better than he was: "I always think, if your students don't know more than you do, don't do better than you, then you're going backwards…. I am more interested in their lives." Similarly, Michael Kleine said,

> What I love the most is when I see my students transcend me and go beyond where I am at. I sometimes don't like the idea of grading papers, but I do like to respond. When I see growth, it is so exhilarating. I mean I really see that growth and change, and I absolutely love that….and that's what I most desire; not to control my students, but to see them be empowered and surpass me.

Valerie Manusov is a final example. Early in the interview, she explained that her interest in communication sparked from caring about how people form relationships. And, as it turns out for her, developing relationships with students was the most meaningful part of being a professor:

> What has been really important for me in my life is my relationships with my graduate students. My relationships with and my ability to be able to help my students over the lifespan of their career, that always felt good. So that was very sustaining for me.

In the end, most of the professors we interviewed found the most value in the relationship that they created with students. They found meaning in being part of students' life-long journey. In their in-depth ethnographic study of college experience, Chambliss and Takacs (2014) found a similar point. As they wrote, "person-to-person relationships are fundamental at every stage" (p. 4) of the university experience. For students, particularly, the relationship with a teacher and mentor was at the heart of a successful and meaningful college experience. It carried a long-lasting impact and shaped the direction of their professional career. This chapter adds another layer to Chambliss and Takacs's work. Relationships are not just meaningful to students. They are also meaningful for teachers who long to be part of a student's life-long journey.

A Movement Toward Hearing Students' Voices

In the preface of his book *Integration of Abilities*, Paul Baker (1977) wrote:

> My strongest feeling about teaching is that you must begin with the student … you do not begin to teach, thinking of your own ego and what you know. You begin with the student and where he is….You don't teach a class. You teach a student. He asks a question—you answer him. (p. xiii)

Paul Baker's (1977) statement about teaching reflected most participants' approach to teaching in later stages of practice. The interviews revealed a movement *toward* this philosophy—very few started there. This approach was well described by Steven Beebe, who said:

> I see my teaching as how can I get messages out of students rather than seeing my job during a class period or even during office hours as lecturing or putting messages into students. The more powerful messages are those that make those connections and I can facilitate that.

For communication professors, learning to teach more effectively involved that transition: to move from speaking to students and covering content, to engaging with students. Carol Thompson, who has actively taught for decades, shared with me: "my teaching has changed from a presentational style to a far more interactive dialogic style." She said: "I am no longer the star of the show. When I presented I was the star, but now you give that up for the greater relationship you are establishing in the dialogic moment." When she described her development about teaching in particular, she explained it in this way:

> I began teaching by emulating the professors....As I learned more about teaching, more of my teaching changed and more of my communication changed. I encountered *The Courage to Teach*, for example, and some of these other deeper explorations of teaching. Then, I started to teach with Michael Kleine and he had me read *Pedagogy of the Oppressed*, and [on] one page it says the teacher teaches and the students are taught. It has a list of all of these things that can be done in teaching and I looked at it and I thought "oh my gosh," I've done some of these things, "oh lord!" That made me think of what was happening because of what the end of Freire's book says about dialogue. Dialogue is what brings people together and the dialogic method of teaching is what really helps students deepen their understanding. [I] started working on this idea of deepening because what I was doing before I thought I was great [but] students would leave that classroom not knowing a thing because all they had done was heard me talk. So I started looking at it from another framework. What do I want them to really know at the end of this? And so this notion of getting them involved started to take root, and so for the last 24 years or so I have been working on getting the ideas to take root and that doesn't involve me dancing around the classroom becoming the focal point. It involves them becoming the focal point and really embracing the ideas and talking about the ideas and making those ideas their own— that's what a good teacher does. I mean, in my mind, how do I get them to make these ideas their own? That shift again is from self-down to other and I think that happens again through growth and longevity and maturity as a person and in the profession.

In her book, Maryellen Weimer (2002) draws on Biggs's research (1999a, 1999b) to describe three distinguishable stages of teacher growth. At the first level, she explained, "the focus is on student differences" (p. 178). At this stage, teachers see the gap between students' performance and believe that if "students do not learn, it is their fault" (p. 178). In the second stage, the teacher looks inward. "The attempt now," Weimer wrote, "is to have a positive impact on student learning with a repertoire of instructional strategies" (p. 178). But the last phase, the focus shifts to student learning. As Biggs (1999b) wrote, "it's not what teachers do, it's what students do that is the important thing" (p. 63). This general growth is what happened to Carol Thompson.

In the interviews, most participants in the study foregrounded that their development moved them toward students. Early in their teaching career, the faculty were focusing on the message—on what to say, on what to do, and on planning. Much later, students became the focus. Jon Nussbaum, who has written extensively on communication across the lifespan (e.g., Nussbaum, 2016), and who "always wanted to be a professor," described his student-focused approach well. For him, the basis of teaching was to find a way to adapt to his audience and to relate to their experiences:

> I had to force myself to watch what they were watching on television or to understand the technology they were using, what their lives were all about. When you get into your '30s, for me I've been teaching for about 10 years. That's when I started realizing that I just didn't understand. There was just a generational change there, and so I had to work extra hard. All of the students were watching *Dawson's Creek*, and so I forced myself to watch it and I can talk about all the different characters on *Dawson's Creek* and made them laugh their butts off because they couldn't imagine me watching that…it's a lot of hard work to make, so that I can get on their level, so that I'm interested in what they're interested in. And of course work that into the context of the class. So I think it becomes harder, you know, and it actually takes more time and you have to understand who you are and the way they look at you.

Maintaining a sense of what students were about was one way to enact a student-centered focus. Get to know your audience, many scholars of communication told us, and they applied it to teaching: get to know your students. This engagement in seeking to understand students—their stories, their likes and dislikes, their passions and hobbies—is a hallmark of faculty teaching in the field of communication. It is probably a ritual that cuts across all programs in the nation: first-day activities to get to know students and for students to get to know each other. Group work that moves students to collaborate and work together. The communication professors we interviewed worked at getting to know their students.

In my interview with Gary Kreps, he described this transition toward a student-focused approach. His teaching experience began as a young master's student at the University of Colorado at Boulder. "I realized that I was acting as a sage on the stage," he said. "I'm doing all the talking," he pointed out. But then, a shift took place in which he put students to work and engaged them in projects. "My goal today," he explained, "is to get students to produce." "I want them to be actively engaged," he emphasized. For most communication professors, there was not a single turning point that could be identified. Rather, they slowly and gradually shifted toward getting students to do the talking. Dan O'Hair, who served as president of the National Communication Association in 2006, echoed Gary Kreps's experience: "I lecture less and interact more," he said. "I enjoy hearing students' voices." The pleasure of teaching became less about speaking and more about listening. And with that perspective in mind, the faculty increasingly fostered experiential learning.

A Movement Toward Experiential Learning

In my interview with Allan Ward (2004), he talked extensively about teaching, learning, and the students he met in the classroom. In one reflection, which aligned well with the title of one of his books, *Postmodern Zen: A Path of Paradox and Process*, he said,

> you know, Julien, it is different to look at a rock on a mountain top that's been there for a thousand years than to bring the rock into the classroom and say "look at this, this was on a mountaintop."

Throughout their professional lifespan, the professors we interviewed moved toward experiential learning—toward creating experiences in or out of the classroom that would require students to be engaged, to experience, or to voice their ideas. They wanted to bring the rock into the classroom.

One way that the faculty moved in that direction was to create an environment in which students engaged in conversations inside the classroom. Stephen Littlejohn, who served as professor of Communication at Humboldt State University and wrote a widely used graduate-level textbook on communication theory (see Littlejohn & Foss, 2011), reflected on his teaching experience in this way:

So when I started teaching, I saw myself as the provider of information. That I came in knowing and students did not know and I was going to teach them what I knew, very didactically. And I remember when I was up for reappointment one time as an assistant professor, we got reviewed every year, and the committee wrote something about my teaching, which made me outraged. That Littlejohn was good but he is over-prepared [laughs]. And I thought, "How can I be over prepared? Preparation is good!" And it took me a few years to realize what they meant by that. I have gained a certain amount of confidence, I have become a more intuitive, more virtuoso teacher, and I realized what they meant. What they meant was, I was too stuck, too rigid. That I would go in with a format and a lesson plan, I was kind of not allowing myself to be creative or to be loose or experiential, in a way. It was about the mid-1980s, it was about the time that I went to UNM that I was starting to get introduced to social constructionism. And I began to have some confidence in my own ideas and myself after several years of teaching. I began to discover that my spontaneous examples were better than my planned examples. And I was beginning to discover that the decisions that I made on the fly in the classroom led to a better outcome than what it was on the lecture notes. So by the end of the 1980s, my teaching got really shifted from much more of a didactic presentational, transitional model of teaching, to much more of a facilitative, experiential one.

Notice that the change does not seem too drastic—faculty and students are still in a classroom and talking is happening. But, Stephen's new approach is a paradigm shift in his way of thinking about the classroom. It is a shift in terms of who is doing the talking and in what way. Stephen has moved toward creating experiential learning with students.

In my interview with Em Griffin, who was an assistant professor 8 years before I was even born, he also described an important shift in his teaching. One course he taught for several years was Group Dynamics—a version of a small group communication class. Consider how he described that shift:

> There was a change in my teaching when I started teaching Group Dynamics to eight students every summer on an island in Lake Michigan. I had two weeks with them, and we studied group dynamics by studying us. Many friendships developed there, many meaningful relationships. Students changed a lot. This was a signal event in my life. This is the essence of experiential learning, and that started happening in about 1975, and I did it for 20 years.

Experiential learning is a change in perspective in the teacher's way of thinking. It is a movement toward student learning. Instead of asking, "What am I going to teach today?" the teacher moves in the direction of asking:

"What will students do today?" "What will facilitate their learning?" The change in the question alters what happens in the classroom—it invites the teacher to reflect more deeply about the kinds of experiences that students need to more fully understand the material. As Gary Kreps shared,

> I try to actively engage my students to participate in the class. So it is not just me talking to them. I try to get them doing projects outside of the classroom…to apply the things we talk about in class.

Similarly, Gerry Philipsen said,

> In my teaching, I have tried over the years to move from the point where I have limited lectures, not to none, but very strategically placed lectures that are very important. The learning of the subject in my view. And to put students to work together in intellectual tasks.

An important way that communication professors created experiential learning was to ask students to engage *interactionally* with others. These interactions could take place inside the classroom by engaging in conversations, in debates, or by working together on small group tasks. But sometimes, as was inspired by Allan Ward, learning could be fostered by inviting students to meet other people outside of the classroom. He said, "I reflected back on classes [and] the more experiences we can give our students in classes, outside the classroom even, will enrich them." Drawing on his own personal story, he explained, "if we can help to provide personally, individually, or in a class situation experiences," then students will learn even more. And so, Allan created those experiences inside the classroom and outside: "I would ask class at times, how many of you at campus here have acquaintances from other countries who are students here? It was usually zero." Speaking to the class, he would add: "between now and the next time, find someone, even if you have to explain to them that you are doing it as a class assignment, and come back and just report about what happened." Allan sought to create conversations that would not have happened without nudging students in that direction.

The point is this: most participants in this study described their teaching as moving in the direction of experiential learning. Experienced professors created learning experiences for students. They engaged students in dialogue, in debate, or in conversations with strangers. They moved away from lecturing or sharing information to fostering critical learning environments.

Conclusion

Teaching excellence is not a state of being. It is a lifelong process of professional development that involves moving away from certain tendencies and moving toward new ways of doing. In this study, we found that communication professors moved in three major directions. First, they increasingly moved toward students and their learning. Early on, the tendency is for the teacher to transmit information and to control the time, the interactions, and the material. With experience, faculty shift toward what students need to learn and become more flexible and fluid. With this shift in mind, they moved from speaking to students to listening to their voices. Finally, they moved toward experiential learning. Throughout their lifespan, thus, communication professors continuously moved in the direction of student learning. They experienced a paradigm shift from an "Instruction Paradigm" to a "Learning Paradigm" (Barr & Tagg, 1995), from teaching content to producing learning.

In a study of the exemplary professors, Silvestri (2005) revealed that two of the most important factors for teaching excellence are love for teaching and learning and respect for students. The third one is to have a student-centered philosophy of teaching and learning. Teaching excellence is all about students. This study adds the fine point that teaching well is a movement rather than an outcome. It is the process of caring more and more about students and their learning. And for many teachers at the latter part of their career, they loved students more than ever. Steve Beebe, for example, said "I love the teaching. It's the connection to the students. It's being involved in changing students' lives. ...And the greatest joy I get is mentoring students." Similarly, Art Bochner, Distinguished University Professor at the University of South Florida, explained,

> One of the reasons I haven't retired at this point is I enjoy it too much. I don't know what I would do without being in the classroom. I could still write and do books and things like that. But I would miss that energy in the classroom.

The love for students is at the heart of teaching. This point is well illustrated by this final story from one of my students. In one assignment, I ask my students to make contact with two communication professors whose work they enjoy. The task is to reach out and to see where the conversation goes. One student contacted Irwin Altman, one of the co-creators of Social Penetration Theory. In class, she shared how she found his phone number and contacted him directly at home. We all giggled at the thought of Carolyn tracking down Altman at his house. The phone rang and a voice picked up. It was an older woman. So then my student asked, "Could I please speak with Mr. Altman?" The voice responded: "I'm sorry, but he is not here right now, can I help you?" And so Carolyn told her, "I'm a student from the University of Arkansas at Little Rock." Before she could even explain the purpose of the call, Altman's wife interrupted her and said, "Oh, you are a student. He loves students so much. He is actually here and nothing would make him happier than to talk to you." Altman got on the phone and they spoke together for 30 minutes, leaving a lifelong joy in my student Carolyn, who had talked to 85-year-old Altman at his home.

References

Bain, K. (2004). *What the best college teachers do.* Cambridge, MA: Harvard University Press.

Baker, P. (1977). *Integration of abilities: Exercises for creative growth.* Anchorage, AK: Anchorage Press.

Barr, R. B., & Tagg, J. (1995). From teaching to learning: A new paradigm for undergraduate education. *Change: The Magazine of Higher Learning, 27*(6), 12–26.

Biggs, J. (1999a). *Teaching for quality learning at university.* Buckingham, England: Open University Press.

Biggs, J. (1999b). What the student does: Teaching for enhanced learning. *Higher Education Research & Development, 18*(1), 57–75.

Biggs, J., & Tang, C. (2007). Teaching for quality learning at university (3rd ed.). New York, NY: McGraw Hill & Open University Press.

Chambliss, D. F., & Takacs, C. G. (2014). *How college works.* Cambridge, MA: Harvard University Press.

Littlejohn, S. W., & Foss, K. A. (2011). *Theories of human communication* (10th ed). Long Grove, IL: Waveland Press.

Marton, F., & Säljö, R. (1976). On qualitative differences in learning: I—Outcome and process. *British Journal of Educational Psychology, 46*(1), 4–11.

Nathan, R. (2006). *My freshman year: What a professor learned by becoming a student.* Chicago, IL: Penguin.

Nussbaum, J. F. (2016). *Communication across the lifespan.* New York, NY: Peter Lang.

Silvestri, J. (2005). Exemplary professors: Factors leading to the development of award-winning teachers. *Update on Research & Leadership, 17*(1), 7–9.

Ward, A. (2004). *Postmodern Zen: A path of paradox and process.* Little Rock, AR: Award Press.

Weimer, M. (2002). *Learner-centered teaching: Five key changes to practice.* San Francisco, CA: Wiley.

· 5 ·

HOW DO COMMUNICATION
PROFESSORS THINK?

I have not seen this former student in a while. Her name is Rhonda, and we're chit-chatting at an alumni event. I ask her how she has been doing and what she has been up to after graduation. She says she misses the department and the learning, but is happy to be back working at the local hospital. I'm surprised, because she joined the department to change her career, but decided instead to return to her original job. I ask about this and she says: "you know, the department was so good to me. What it did for me is to take my black and white mind and make it become gray."

In his work on students' growth and development in college, Perry (1999) proposed a model of intellectual development in which students increasingly allowed their minds to become more flexible. At the earliest stages of intellectual development, students tend to see an object of study in simple terms; something is black or white, right or wrong, and authorities have the answers. As students dive into the material and deepen their learning, they move toward multiplicity. They begin to see a diversity of perspectives, that authorities on a subject frequently disagree, and realize that everyone's opinion is equal. As they progress, students learn to see even more: context matters and evidence is an important way of supporting "truth." They move from having an opinion to developing an informed point of view. In this phase, then, students learn to create meaning. According to Perry, a student's development culminates in what he described as "commitment." Commitment in intellectual development is acceptance of the gray area, but also recognizing that action and choices can be made in spite of relativity. This is what happened to Rhonda's mind—it moved from being black and white to being gray.

In this chapter, I explore the ways in which our communication scholars developed their thinking throughout their career. We asked them specific questions about how their thinking about communication changed during their professional career, focusing especially from the time they encountered the field until the present day. We inquired about key ideas and concepts that made a difference in their thinking. We also asked about any stages they saw in their meta-intellectual development. Overall, it was difficult for participants to analyze their own patterns of thinking over time, especially in this impromptu interview. Yet, we found two major themes of cognitive development across their professional career. The first one echoed the work of Perry. Throughout their career, the participants in this study moved from a black and white mind to a gray one. They moved from dualism to commitment. Second, and related, they increasingly committed to a constitutive view of communication. This chapter provides evidence for these two developments and cues how slow intellectual development really is.

From Dualism to Commitment

William Perry's (1999) model of intellectual and ethical development provides a useful scheme for reflecting about how the mind develops. This section introduces it more formally.

According to Perry (1999), *Dualism* is where learners begin: there are right and wrong answers and all problems are solvable. Our thinking about issues, problems, or our discipline is understood as right or wrong, true or false, with a low tolerance for alternatives. Then, we move toward *Multiplicity*. Here, we attempt "to account for diversity in human opinion, experience, and 'truth'" (Perry, 1974, p. 3). There is an increasing acceptance in uncertainty and opening of possible alternatives. But, the learner believes that "there are obviously right ways, or methods, to find the right answers." The third movement is *Contextual Relativism*. This transition "represents a fundamental transformation of one's perspective—from a vision of the world as essentially dualistic …to a vision of a world as essentially relativistic and context-bound with a few right/wrong exceptions" (Hofer & Pintrich, 2002, p. 21). The fourth phase is *Commitment*, in which the individual "define[s] one's identity in a contextually relativistic world (p. 21)." The general movement of Perry's model is to move "from a passive receptor of facts to an active agent in defining arguments and creating new knowledge" (p. 22). In our interviews, our participants described this progression—they saw themselves as moving toward complexity, toward seeing alternative perspectives, and ultimately, for some of them, committing to a way of being and thinking.

My interview with Valerie Manusov exemplifies Perry's model of intellectual development. I asked her: "How has your thinking about communication changed over the years?" She answered first by describing a movement away from basic research. "Let's understand this thing," she said, "with the presumption that was going to be important, but not thinking that much about the social importance." Increasingly, she moved toward another question. "Why does it matter? Why is this important?" Then, she explained how her thinking changed:

> One of the biggest changes has been that the nature of my questions has changed. I think it has become more interesting because I actually really really, really care about the answer. And I also moved away from the simplistic responses, so I kind of like to say "okay, there is a dark side to this and there is a beneficial side to this." And bringing that out to not make it all like, "if you do all this, it would be good" because life is just not seen as that, relationships are not seen as that.

Valerie's work has now moved in a different direction as she is investigating mindfulness in relationships (e.g., Knowles, Manusov, & Crowley, 2015). In describing her new research focus, she acknowledged the inherent complexities. "A lot of things I am reading," she said, "are about how beneficial it is and it generally is." At the same time,

> The more mindful that you are or the more time that you spend in silence, the more you realize that there are things about yourself or your relationships that you don't like and it can take you to a really dark place. And it can lead you to break up your relationship. It's not like "if you can do this, everything will get better."

And to that end, she said, "When I was younger, I liked simplicity and easier answers. I liked the world a little bit more black and white and neat."

Our scholars moved toward complexity. They sought to discover multiple truths and recognized the complexities of human communication. This point is well noted by Robert Craig, professor emeritus at the University of Colorado at Boulder. Bob has written extensively about communication as a discipline. In fact, in one ground-breaking article, he provided a scheme for organizing the field in distinctive modes of thought and conversations (see Craig, 1999) and called communication scholars to think of communication as a practical discipline (see Craig, 1989). In the interview, he explained that there is not just one way of communicating well.

> We need to realize that people engage with each other in different ways. And there can be a lot of good ways of doing it. And what's important is to be engaged with other people, be open to what they're saying, [and] to be interested in learning from them.

There was an expansion in their understanding and a sense of comfort about not knowing. Lynn Turner, for example, spoke about how her understanding of family shifted over the years and about the challenge of defining what a family is. Lynn's scholarship, in fact, focuses on family communication. She is the co-editor of *The Family Communication Sourcebook* (see Turner & West, 2006) and co-author with Richard West of the popular textbook, *Perspectives on Family Communication* (see Turner & West, 2007). From her vantage point, the difficulty lied in matching an expanded view of family with the practical elements of doing research. "The family," she said, "is portrayed in a biogenetic way in research. So that's kind of an ongoing struggle to reconcile the way I think about the topic and the way I do research on it." In fact, even her approach to research expanded as she moved from quantitative to qualitative work (a pattern that was common across our scholars). And even on that point, she described a gradual understanding of what qualitative work is. Consistently in her talk, she used phrases to cue her ongoing growth: "I can see more of a range," "I am starting to think," or "I am starting to see," she said. Consider these phrases in this longer excerpt:

> Initially I thought about qualitative work very similar to quantitative work except without numbers, looking for themes, not necessarily counting anything. And that is a part of qualitative work. But now I see a lot more of the range of how you can do qualitative work. And just looking at some of the more unique things [and] looking at performances. I don't necessarily do those in my own work, but I can see more of a range, more of a way to think about things from a qualitative perspective that really is decidedly different. It's not just trying to get people to talk to you rather than just fill out a questionnaire that you can quantify. It is, I mean, I obviously knew this before, but I think teaching it repeatedly has brought it home to me more vividly. And also

in the way I'm doing my own research now. The more epistemological and ontological and epistemological differences between the two approaches. I used to think one person could do both in one study. And now I'm sort of moving just a bit away from that. You could partner with somebody if you wanted to have multi-methods and crossing quantitative and qualitative. But I am starting to think, as people have told me in the past and I have rejected it, but I am starting to see that if you really believe in a quantitative mindset, it would be hard to apply yourself to qualitative methods and vice versa.

Lynn Turner's personal development as a researcher moved from certainty to uncertainty. It involved changing her methodological approach, expanding her definition of family, and understanding her research with more depth and nuance. Even though Lynn Turner has been a communication researcher for over 25 years, she is still in the process of thinking more clearly, of seeing differently, and of learning anew. I think it is with this perspective that Raymie McKerrow, recipient of the Lifetime Achievement Award from the Critical and Cultural Studies Division at our national conference, said: "I have gained a great deal of humility about what I do not know across those years…I think it is what keeps driving me forward in terms of learning."

Ultimately though, as Perry pointed out in his scheme of intellectual development, the learner makes certain commitments in spite of alternative perspectives. Even though Lynn Turner moved from quantitative to qualitative, for example, she committed to a communication framework. She said, "One of the things that has motivated me as I've done this work is trying to keep a very steady focus on interaction." Some scholars committed to a methodology and others to a particular object of study. Carol Thompson discussed her own growth as moving toward commitment. She said, "I started out with certainty." Then, she described the multiple ideas she encountered: the concept of rhetoric, Aristotle's virtue ethics, and Quintilian. Then, she said, "I was confronted with a multiplicity of stuff that I wasn't prepared for." "Whoa!" she said while moving her head and body like she had been splashed by a bucket of water, "so maybe this plethora of ideas, the multiplicity of ideas that are out there led to a narrowing…a contextual narrowing." "And then finally," she added, "a designation, a decision about what seems to work for me in my thinking and my way of being." She paused.

"And that's when I came to this idea of social construction." She paused again. "We do create a reality by our actions and how we communicate with others, and it's very uncertain." Carol went from certainty to uncertainty and then to commitment. She said, "so you go from certainty to all these multiple ideas looking at it through a context and then finally you've made a decision to commit to something." "I have committed to social construction," she said as her hands moved back closer to her body and her voice lowered.

In the course of their career, our communication scholars moved from dualism to commitment. They felt more comfortable with uncertainty, with the multiplicity of ideas and perspectives, and found their voice. Perry's model has often been applied to undergraduate students, a "population rarely reflecting post-contextual-relativistic thinking" (Hofer & Pintrich, 2002, p. 21). What we can see in the data is that Perry's scheme of intellectual development is a lifelong process. Our communication professionals were still learning to think more clearly and to position themselves in an ocean of ideas. And still, they found a boat of their own and committed to an idea. And sometimes, as we will see below, they all met to ride a new wave of thinking.

From Transmission to Constitution

As we saw above, communication professors' ways of thinking became more gray. They welcomed uncertainty and saw communication as a complex process. In addition, as I explore in this section, their thinking about communication naturally aligned with the metatheoretical development of the field—they moved from seeing communication as transmission to seeing it as a constitutive process whereby social realities are constructed.

In a landmark article, Craig (1999), a participant in this study, described a paradigm shift that was occurring in the field of communication: a movement from thinking about communication as transmission to seeing communication as a constitutive process. By definition, the transmission model of communication is "a process of sending and receiving messages or transferring information from one mind to another" (p. 125). The model flourished post World War II, when Shannon and Weaver (1948) published A *Mathematical Theory of Communication*, in which they described the process of communication as moving from a sender to a receiver. To complete the communication process, Shannon and Weaver suggested, the receiver provides feedback and it closes the loop. In addition, their model proposed that the transmission of information can be interrupted by external noise. The concepts of "sender" and "receiver," as well as the notion of "encoding and decoding messages" and "feedback" and "noise," all contributed to a way of thinking about what communication is. In fact, many people think about communication as a mode of transmission.

But, as Craig (1999) wrote, "the transmission model of communication has come under attack in recent years" (p. 125). The transmission model "is philosophically flawed, fraught with paradox, and ideologically backward" (p. 125), he added. The model that emerged instead is called the constitutive model. From this perspective, "communication is a constitutive process that produces and reproduces shared meaning" (p. 125). The constitutive model, for instance, implies that social reality is co-created in and through communication. Our identities, our relationships, and our social systems are reflected by and constituted through human interaction. Throughout their careers, the participants in our study moved in that direction: from thinking about communication as a mode of transmission to thinking about it as a constitutive process.

For many participants, this shift in their thinking was clear. Dawn O. Braithwaite, for example, said, "I believe communication constitutes relationships, selves, communities, and cultures, organizations. It is the center point of who people are, how they become who they are, and what their experiences are." Then, Dawn explained this shift as a historical development in the field:

> So believing that and not understanding it at the beginning, that didn't even match the communication model we had when I first came into the field. [We] had this very simplistic model, but still, even the idea of feedback was amazing, that is what I teach my students...today it is probably a big "duh," but at the time it was sort of revolutionary to think that communication is not a straight line, it is a loop. And that people are senders and receivers simultaneously and all those ideas really resonated with me. I was like "OK, this is how communication works."

In her work, in fact, Dawn drew on this understanding to shape new thinking about family communication (e.g., Braithwaite & Baxter, 2006). Gerry Philipsen, whose interest in the field began by exploring the process of interaction in small groups, described it in a similar way and pointed out a key reading that moved him in that direction:

> I fell into a course on group discussion with a book titled *The Dynamics of Discussion*, and that book introduced me to a different way of thinking about communication from debate and oratory, thinking of communication as a more cooperative kind of process. ...Communication is something that not only reflects or facilitates commonality and communal life, but it is also something that can constitute it. That it has a constitutive power, it is something that we can bring about and define, a locally distinctive sense of commonality.

Thinking about communication as a constitutive process fundamentally changed our scholars' ways of understanding human interaction. Stephen Littlejohn made this point clear:

> I think I have broadened an understanding of communication not as transmission of information, but the use of speech in communication forms can do something other than transmitting information. I mean that is huge for me in my shift of understanding over the years.

Betsy Bach told me, "We are constantly constructing and responding to definitions of ourselves, and definitions of the other every time we communicate." Similarly, Larry Frey, professor at the University of Colorado at Boulder, whose expertise focuses on communication activism (e.g., Frey & Carragee, 2007a, 2007b) and group communication (Frey, 2006a, 2006b), explained this cognitive shift as a turning point:

> When I first started, the understanding of communication primarily was the transfer of information. And things were approached in that matter. And one significant turning point was the notion that communication is constitutive. It is not just a tool that people use in their relationships, but it is the means by which they relationships are formed.

A relationship, then, is not something people *have*; it is something they *do*. And that way of thinking changes everything.

Michael Kleine spoke of the implications of this shift on the process of relating. Drawing on the concept of rhetoric, he said, "You've probably heard of some of these theorists, Carl Rogers or Kenneth Burke." He paused, and then he said, "so the emphasis on that mode of rhetoric is not so much on being right and winning an argument, it's more on compromise and movement." This time he made a longer pause and spoke more slowly. "A relational movement. Rather than just saying 'you need to just change and be right,'" he said more quickly, "it's more like 'alright how can we change together?' How can we build something together?"

Michael Kleine's point is grounded in Coordinated Management of Meaning (CMM). By definition, CMM suggests that people in interaction co-create social reality. In their work, Pearce and Pearce (2000) argued that "the *form* [emphasis added] of communication, fully as much as the context of what we say, sustains or destroys our personalities, relationships, and institutions" (p. 413). One way of communicating more effectively, the authors suggested, is to ask a fundamental question: "What are we co-constructing together?" (p. 410). As our participants described moving from transmission to constitution, they applied this thinking to practice. Gary Kreps applied it to health communication. He said that he was trying to figure out "how to use conjoint communication with people to reduce uncertainty and develop intelligence in dealing with different situations." Michael Kleine applied it to teaching. "Teachers," he said, "don't own knowledge; it is co-constructed" with students. And Arvind Singhal, who was greatly influenced by Everett Rogers, created a new life script.

"I am focusing on the quality of interaction among us," he told me. "Which includes the quality of who you are and what you bring." He pressed on: "So, it's a trust in the principle of co-creation and it has to be dynamic because it is unfolding organically." After providing some examples, he concluded his point: "So your script will develop, but it will develop in the moment and you will have the faith and confidence that you never really control that script. You co-create it."

"Communication," Glenn, LeBaron, and Mandelbaum (2003) wrote, "is the primary means whereby social realities, cultural contexts, and the meanings of messages are interactively accomplished and experienced" (p. 21). In our interviews, and in the course of their professional lives, our scholars embraced this way of thinking. In conjunction with the discipline, they moved away from thinking about communication as a mode of transmission and toward seeing it as a constitutive process. As they made the leap, there was no turning back. As Valerie Manusov put it, "now it's impossible for me to see things outside of that framework."

Conclusion

The Indian thinker Krishnamurti (1992) once said that "our thinking is the outcome of our own very limited experience." This chapter explored the thinking of communication professionals over the lifespan. Intellectual development, I showed, is a lifelong project, not a learning curve that takes place within the constraints of a time capsule. Our scholars slowly moved from dualism to commitment. They began with certainty and the expectation that knowledge is a state of being rather than a process. As they experienced new ideas and ways of thinking, they found their own voice and took a stance. One change was the influence of the constitutive view of communication with which came the possibility of creating social reality and improving communication as a practice. But, more importantly, they remained open to change and learning.

In approaching the interviews, I was hoping to dive deeply into communication professionals' ways of thinking. For most participants, however, reflecting about the development of their own thinking proved difficult. This is fair: how can you analyze the processes of your own thinking over time? Clearly, my expectations were high. I was also expecting to take note of common theories and concepts that had influenced their development. Some theories were mentioned, of course, but it was not concepts that influenced people the most. It was people.

Even in the life of thinking, which many imagine as a solitary quest, it was people who had made their mark. It was mentors who had invested time and energy or a meeting at a conference that influenced a methodological change. Concepts and ideas do not stand their ground or persuade—it was people who nudged, encouraged, or inspired. The life of learning, then, is not a life of solitude, but of relationship and connection. Allan Ward, as always, put it best:

> I pay attention to the new things I haven't discovered yet. I get up thinking this is a new day, a new sunrise, and something could happen today that could be insight into something that I just haven't dreamed of before. So every person I meet is like a person that has a message from the universe to me, and I want to be sensitive and alert to that.

Rhonda's mind did not shift from being black and white to gray through concepts—it moved from the communication teachers around her who cared to influence her. Ideas are important, but it is people who matter more.

References

Braithwaite, D. O., & Baxter, L. A. (2006). *Engaging theories in family communication: Multiple perspectives*. Thousand Oaks, CA: Sage.

Craig, R. T. (1989). Communication as a practical discipline. In B. Dervin, L. Grossberg, B. O'Keefe, & E. Wartella (Eds.), *Rethinking communication; Volume 1: Paradigm issues* (pp. 97–122). Newbury Park, CA: Sage.

Craig, R. T. (1999). Communication theory as a field. *Communication Theory*, 9(2), 119–161.

Frey, L. R. (Ed.). (2006a). *Facilitating group communication in context: Innovations and applications with natural groups: Vol. 1. Facilitating group creation, conflict, and communication*. Cresskill, NJ: Hampton Press.

Frey, L. R. (Ed.). (2006b). *Facilitating group communication in context: Innovations and applications with natural groups: Vol. 2. Facilitating group task and team communication*. Cresskill, NJ: Hampton Press.

Frey, L. R., & Carragee, K. M. (Eds.). (2007a). *Communication activism: Volume 1. Communication for social change*. Cresskill, NJ: Hampton Press.

Frey, L. R., & Carragee, K. M. (Eds.). (2007b). *Communication activism: Volume 2. Media and performance activism*. Cresskill, NJ: Hampton Press.

Glenn, P., LeBaron, C., & Mandelbaum, J. (Eds.) (2003). *Studies in language and social interaction: In honor of Robert Hopper*. Mahwah, NJ: Lawrence Erlbaum.

Hofer, B. K., & Pintrich, P. R. (Eds.). (2002). *Personal epistemology: The psychology of beliefs about knowledge and knowing*. New York, NY: Routledge.

Knowles, J. H., Manusov, V., & Crowley, J. (2015). Minding your matters: Predicting satisfaction, commitment, and conflict strategies from trait mindfulness. *Interpersonal: An International Journal on Personal Relationships, 9*(1), 44–58.

Krishnamurti, J. (1992). *On relationship*. New York, NY: HarperCollins.

Pearce, W. B., & Pearce, K. A. (2000). Extending the theory of the coordinated management of meaning (CMM) through a community dialogue process. *Communication Theory, 10*(4), 405–423.

Perry, W. G. (1974). *Students as makers of meaning*. Annual report of the Bureau of Study Counsel, Harvard University. Retrieved from http://bsc.harvard.edu/

Perry, W. G. (1999). *Forms of intellectual and ethical development in the college years: A scheme*. San Francisco, CA: Jossey-Bass.

Shannon, C. E., & Weaver, W. (1948). *A mathematical theory of communication*. Urbana, IL: University of Illinois Press.

Turner, L. H., & West, R. (Eds.). (2006). *The family communication sourcebook*. Thousand Oaks, CA: Sage.

Turner, L. H., & West, R. (2007). *Perspectives on family communication* (3rd ed.). New York, NY: McGraw Hill.

· 6 ·

WHAT DO COMMUNICATION
PROFESSORS SEE AND HEAR?

A few years ago, I met a colleague on campus whose expertise was in birds. I found it fascinating that he could be walking on campus, hear a bird call and be able to identify the species, the sex, and the function of various calls. His knowledge enabled him to experience a different reality than I would. All I could do, I thought to myself, is enjoy the singing. This conversation inspired me to do some research on a red bird I see frequently outside my home: the red robin.

When I searched to understand more, I first found that my description was inaccurate; the bird is actually called a Northern Cardinal. Its colors, the flashing red on the body, the little bit of black around the eyes, and the purple on its tail, mark that it is a male rather than a female. The female, in fact, is smaller and colored with grays and browns. Northern Cardinals have a variety of calls, some for mating and some to protect their territory. For example, if the whistle sounds like, "cheeeer-a-dote, cheeer-a-dote-dote-dote, purdy, purdy, purdy … whoit, whoit, whoit, whoit, what-cheer, what-cheer … wheet, wheet, wheet, wheet," then it is designed to warn other birds that they are encroaching on an existing territory. I also discovered, to my surprise, that Northern Cardinals often find a single mate for life. Of course, my knowledge of Northern Cardinals is limited, but a few facts have raised my ability to appreciate this wonderful bird and to understand this part of reality in a more complex way. And that is what learning is all about.

Disciplinary knowledge, whether it is biology or communication, gives a person a way of understanding and interpreting reality. Theories and concepts, in fact, provide a perceptual lens through which to interpret and understand some aspects of the world: birds, stars, or human interaction. In this chapter, I describe what communication professors see in, and understand about, the social world. Among other questions, I ask: What do they notice? What do they pay attention to? What does their discipline enable them to experience and understand?

In the interviews, our communication professors reported seeing three dominant points of attention: nonverbal communication, verbal communication, and the many missed opportunities for connection in interaction. To proceed, the chapter begins by explaining the nature of professional vision. The rest of the chapter describes the three aspects mentioned above; how they see small, and often taken-for-granted, nonverbal behaviors, the ways they see language in use and its various functions, and the problems that are created in human interaction and the opportunities to connect that laypersons miss.

The Nature of Professional Vision

What does an archeologist see when they look at soil? What does an expert in police use of force see when they examine the beating of Rodney King? And what can we learn from these professionals about how communication scholars see the world around them?

In one article on professional vision, Goodwin (1994) answered the first two questions. He argued that in every profession, people have discursive tools, or ways of talking, to make sense of the reality that they are exploring. Specifically, he proposed three unique concepts that professionals use to interpret reality: highlighting, inscription, and coding schemes. For the purposes of this chapter, I focus here on the last one: the nature of coding schemes.

As Goodwin (1994) defined it, coding "transforms phenomena observed in a specific setting in the objects of knowledge that animate the discourse of a profession" (p. 606). Linguists, he explained, "classify sounds in terms of phonetic distinctions" and "sociologists classify people according to sex and class" (p. 608). Professionals often have tools that enable them to code their subject. When archeologists examine dirt, for instance, they use the Munsell color chart. The chart provides a tool through which to examine the dirt in terms of color, consistency, and texture. So, archaeologists can build on previous theoretical knowledge that is synthesized in the chart and compare it to the soil they are examining. The chart thus provides a coding scheme through which to interpret the soil, and the tool shapes the archeologist's vision.

Professional knowledge functions in a similar way. Theories and concepts enable professionals or new learners to see the world anew; to code what they see or experience in light of the abstract knowledge they are taught. In the field of communication, for instance, if a student learns the concept of face-threat or face-attack (see Tracy & Tracy, 1998), they can apply that concept to human interaction. With a definition, they will learn to understand that a face-threat is any speech act that damages the positive or negative face of a hearer or speaker; that is, any utterance that threatens a person's sense of competency, autonomy, or need to be loved and respected. With this knowledge, they can then interpret people's conversational moves in light of that concept.

In their research on 911 phone calls, Tracy and Tracy (1998) offered several examples of face-threatening acts. In one case, a caller asks "How long do I have to wait though?" The response from the call-taker is this: "Until SOMEBODY GETS THERE. You're not listening. I can't tell you any better than that." Viewed from the perspective of the concept of face-threat, the call-taker is damaging the positive face of the caller. This is done first by speaking loudly and second by straightforwardly accusing the other of not listening. This is a simple example, but the point is that concepts and theoretical constructs about communication can shape a person's vision and understanding of what is taking place during interaction. To return to Goodwin's point, communication theory and concepts, thus, are coding schemes that inform our scholars' professional vision.

In my interviews with participants, I did not inquire about their professional vision. I did not ask how discourse analysts analyze talk or how quantitative researchers examine complex data, or how they use theory to code empirical data. That is a form of professional vision too. I asked participants to reflect on what they saw and experienced as communication professionals in real-life interactions. What do they see and hear that other people who have not been trained in communication cannot see or hear? The rest of the chapter answers this question in light of three dominant coding schemes: (a) nonverbal communication, (b) verbal communication, and (c) the process of co-construction.

Nonverbal Communication

When I was in my teens, we lived in a house in a French village of 200 people, with the church situated at the crossroads of two main streets. The street we lived on was a row of more modern homes, bordered by an immense forest, in which my friends and I disappeared over the weekend. At this point, my father was an insurance salesman in Switzerland and would travel back and forth through the border. To prepare for his interactions, he read avidly in the area of nonverbal communication with the goal of seeing how his clients were behaving, and to give himself an advantage in the interaction. While reading several books on the topic, he would share what he had learned at the dinner table. For example, he told us, "when a person is touching or scratching their nose, they may be exaggerating a story or lying. When a person is scratching their head," he would say, "they might be frustrated or irritated by a comment that was just made." Since then, I have never forgotten these two nonverbal behaviors and their possible meanings. I can watch an interaction and see these behaviors when they occur and have some interpretive potential for understanding what they mean. Knowing about the possible interpretation of these two gestures changed what I saw in human interactions. In my interviews, many participants spoke about the ability to see, interpret, and understand the many nonverbal cues that most people do not focus on, nor interpret consciously.

Communication scholars can see nonverbal communication in action. By definition, nonverbal communication includes how people use space, gestures, or touch. It also involves how individuals use facial expressions, make eye contact, as well as how they speak—the rate of talk, the accent, and the use of pauses (see Knapp, Hall, Horgan, 2013). All of these features are a fundamental part of the complex process of human communication. Nonverbal communication is also an inherent part of our scholars' theoretical knowledge, and, in turn, a coding scheme that informed their professional vision.

Many participants in our study explained that they consciously see and interpret complex cues as interaction unfolds. Consider, for example, Allan Ward's reflections:

> I find that it's like having a sixth sense where often I get an inkling of something before I'm conscious of what it is. And that it's not so much a constant investigation, but a realization from verbal, from words, from the nonverbal communication on how things are said and so on….I just discover it and so once I realized in the study of it that, for example, with people the eye dilates and constricts continuously, and the

words can cause a dilation if we like it and close it out if we don't. We are seeing all of this in everyone we are talking to all the time. I find that I'll walk across campus now, and just passing someone, it's like there's a whole array of information that's coming concerning the walk, the slouch, the shoulders, the size of the stride, what they're looking at, if they're on a cell phone, if they're looking up, if they look like death warmed over or if there's something eagerly that they seem to be hidden to. All those things are happening constantly so there's a wealth of information constantly.

A few comments later, Allan reflected back on this section and added:

We can be much more alert to information that is all around us, that we, under other circumstances, might not be aware of, and then becoming conscious of things sometimes after the fact, you know, I'll find something will happen in the morning and in the evening, I think back, "Oh, that's what was happening there!"

Many participants in the study found the details of nonverbal communication fascinating. Early on in his career, for example, Dan O'Hair wrote extensively about the nature of deception and nonverbal communication (e.g., Cody & O'Hair, 1983). In the interview, he said "one of my favorite studies that I have ever conducted were on nonverbal behavior, whether it is body movement or whether it is vocalic, rhythm, speed, or rate." Notice here the variety of layers that he describes, the subtleties of the paralinguistic features of talk. John Peters, whose research seeks to understand communication "in its broad historical, legal, philosophical, religious, and technological context," essentially echoed Dan's comment: "I see lots of things. Tone of voice, posture, chair position, are my legs crossed? I try to watch the other and kind of observe what they're doing." John Daly said "I notice more about the way people communicate. I am more analytical about the way they do things. I notice where people sit in meetings for example." Gary Kreps shared Dan's enthusiasm. "I love to watch people," he told me. "I love to watch the way people interact." He further explained: "I am very interested in particularly looking at a lot of the ways that they display themselves nonverbally. So I am very aware of those things and I focus on them." With this answer, I probed more deeply and asked him what he could see and hear that someone untrained may not see and hear. He responded, "I can often see based on whether they are leaning towards each other, whether they are providing eye contact, matching facial expressions, paralinguistic cues. I can always tell what the nature of the relationship is."

When Kristina Godfrey, my graduate student, interviewed Jon Nussbaum, his reply focused on whether people are listening. He said, "There are so many distractions, so I'm hyper aware that I am focused on that person I'm talking to, so I easily notice when cell phones are going off or when people aren't paying attention." Nussbaum's research focus, in fact, informed his ways of seeing and thinking (see e.g., Nussbaum, Federowicz, & Nussbaum, 2009; Nussbaum, Miller-Day, & Fisher, 2009). He explained,

> since I deal with older adults in my research, I'm very much aware of physiological changes, so is this person actually hearing me?...Are they hearing what I am saying? Do they have any kind of emotional issue? So what's going on in their lives that are causing these problems?

A person's research endeavor, in fact, informed the focus of that person's seeing. Much like Jon Nussbaum, Kristine Muñoz's research in language and social interaction directed her attentiveness: "Accents, face-threats, sequential organization, gender dynamics and racial dynamics, culture like 'Only an American could have said!' or 'How Colombian was that?'" I probed again and she added: "I can tell you who is interrupting, who is being interrupted. I can tell you when someone's accent has just gotten thicker or has disappeared, often where it is from, the dialect feature that is shared among others in the group."

One distinguishing feature of experts and non-experts is not just that they saw more behaviors. They also realized the complexity of interaction and that what they saw and paid attention to was in fact only a portion of the possibilities. More behaviors are produced in a 30-second encounter than people can pay attention to (Streeck, Goodwin, LeBaron, 2011; Streeck & Mehus, 2005). The human face alone is capable of making some 250,000 different expressions (Birdwhistell, 1970). Wendy Leeds-Hurwitz spoke to this and in fact quoted Ray Birdwhistell, one of the first researchers on nonverbal communication. She said that she has "a little bit more ability to see things deliberately." I asked, "well, okay, tell me more about that." This is what she said:

> Birdwhistell always told us that there were 2000 separate things you could do. If we were researching, there were 2000 separate things we could note about what somebody did with their body. And obviously, we can't pay attention to that many things on purpose. So what happens is people notice things that stand out to them and you may notice a very, very, very tiny percentage of that whole. Birdwhistell noticed much more than most of us. I think what happened as I've gotten older and maybe more skilled is that I notice a bit more deliberately and can react to it deliberately.

Nonverbal communication was one aspect of communication that the professors we interviewed paid attention to. They reflected on their ability to see nonverbal actions *in situ*, and interpreted various meanings out of what they saw. This interpretative potential gave them a strength. As Gary Kreps explained,

> It gives me great advantages because I can understand a lot of times what people are looking for and why things are working the way they are and I can try to adapt my behavior. It also gives me a lot of insight into trying to improve communication.

At the same time, the faculty realized the limitations of interpreting non-verbal communication. As Valerie Manusov put it, "I notice more things in the small behaviors that people exhibit but I do not ever, almost ever, jump to the interpretation of it….I know that any behavior can mean so many different things." But, she added, "I will ask questions or will make observations that are usually based on seeing." The professors in this study could see non-verbal communication in action, but they added the important lesson about not jumping to conclusions.

Communication involves more than gesturing, moving in space, touching, or leaning. People also use words and language to share meaning. As such, many professors reflected on their abilities to see interaction in light of the ways people spoke. I focus on this point next.

Verbal Communication

My first interviewee was Carol Thompson, my colleague who has been in the department since the early 1990s. She served as department chair for many years and was a founding director of the Academy for Teaching and Learning Excellence on campus. In the 12 years that I have been in the department, I have rarely heard Carol criticize anyone. She is constantly highlighting the positive, complimenting, giving support, or simply being present. We are sitting in her office amidst the memorabilia she has collected over the years, including many books, which she loves dearly. In our conversation, I asked her about what she saw and experienced while being in interaction. She said,

> Everything you've mentioned I see. At the grocery store, you see how the boss talks to the cashier and you see the disconfirmation there, or the disconfirmation to the cashier or to the waitress or whatever or you see parents talking to children, and you go, "what are you constructing here with your communication?"

She added very softly, but assertively: "I see it everywhere. I can look at a group of people and tell who is on the inside and who is on the outside. I can just see it."

Like Carol, many of the communication professors in the study saw verbal communication in action. They paid attention to language-in-use, to word choices, and to the impact that messages had on the people involved in the interaction. Larry Frey, who co-authored a powerful book about the interactional dynamics of people living together with AIDS (see Adelman & Frey, 1997), prefaced his response by saying: "I don't think people are always very clear about the intent of their message." Amanda Pasierb, who conducted this interview, asked him to explain. This is what he said:

> People often hide the intent. For example, if they say something like "Why do you do that? Why do you do X or Y or Z?" Quite often what they're really trying to say is "I'm concerned about you, and that's the reason for asking about that, that I would like to help." But notice that they don't articulate those particular statements. So I think one thing we can do is point to the deeper intent or meaning, or really foreground the most important kinds of things that need to get across in statements.

How people express themselves is puzzling. As Michel Foucault (quoted in Dreyfus & Rabinow, 1982) once explained, "People know what they do; they frequently know why they do what they do; but what they don't know is what what they do does" (p. 187). Although Foucault was right about the average person, he is not correct about most communication professionals. When Larry Frey hears a question, he actually hears the potentiality of a statement. Take John Peters, professor at the University of Iowa, as another example: "I am really sensitive to speech acts. I think I really notice what people are doing with words. I think that most people don't realize, always, how they're operating with words." Communication professionals do think about what messages do, their functions and consequences. Dan O'Hair, for instance, said, "We are hyper sensitive to not only messages but what are the responses to messages, whether they would be mediated or conversational. I think we do wonder about audience effects, whether the audience is one or one hundred."

In seeing how verbal messages operate, communication professionals often see problems, how conflict emerges, or the making of dysfunctional patterns. Gary Kreps, for example, said:

> One of the things that I can often see is the ways that different levels of messages either work together or work against one another. And so I am particularly interested in looking at the ways that those message systems do not fit very, very well and usually

that will tell me about tension, will tell me about subterfuge, it will tell me about uncertainty. So I am very sensitive to looking at the interplay between different levels and types of messages and how to design systems to try to be better at communication.

A little bit later, after several questions, Gary added, "I can see a lack of convergence between messages and communicators."

Tom Socha, who is leading a positive communication movement in the field (see Socha & Beck, 2015), also spoke about the various messages that he heard. He said:

I see and hear, well especially because my interest area has been families and children for most of my career, I hear a lot about bad parenting. I hear a lot of messages that I hear parents giving their children …. I can see where they have given these messages before, have a sense of where that's going to take them. I have to resist being an interventionist and sometimes I say "well, here is a suggestion you might want to say this," or "here is another idea, here is another way of doing it or model it, you know, something different."

Professors of communication saw how people communicated verbally—the way they talked and their word choices. But often, those choices were seen in light of a larger context: the group, the relationship, the organization, or the conflict. With the influence of Barnett Pearce and his theory of Coordinated Management of Meaning (see Pearce & Pearce, 2000), Stephen Littlejohn, for example, explained that he saw relationships in the making:

For me, what I see is a process in which people are negotiating or working out a relationship. What that means is I am not just hearing words or hearing a message. I am not just looking at styles or qualities of communicators; I am actually looking at how are these people negotiating or constructing their relationship... so what I see is how those forms of interaction are making relationship or a social world in which they both live. So the same thing holds when I am working with groups and individuals in the community. If I am doing a mediation, for example, where many mediators could primarily see a conflict and they see an opportunity to resolve that conflict. So they are seeing conflict resolution and all the parts of conflict and resolution. But I see how those people are communicating. How can I work with them to change their forms of communication, so that the relationship is transformed in a way that they can join and decide what kind of relationship they want for themselves and I think that is a bit different from the average person.

Karen Foss, a rhetorician at heart, highlighted a similar message: "I see and hear people creating worlds that they may not want to be creating, but do not realize what they are doing." The point is this: communication scholars can see and hear verbal communication in light of the knowledge they have acquired in the discipline. They see and hear speech acts, face-threats, interruptions, the identity and relational functions of talk, and the ways in which people are creating their relationship and local contexts through communication. To draw on Michel Foucault again, communication professionals can see and hear "what what people do does." And this gives them the power to see where the opportunities for change are.

(Missed) Opportunities

Communication professors' ways of seeing and hearing often called them to see the missed opportunities in everyday interaction. They saw both actuality and potentiality. They experienced human interaction, not just by seeing what was happening, but also by contrasting it in their mind with what could be done differently. For many, there is a great potential for people to interact differently. In that realization lied both sadness about how things are, but joy about how things could be. This idea was well expressed in my first interview with Carol:

> I can only take care of [myself]. If the patron treats the cashier badly, all I can do is make eye contact and smile and ask how everything is going for you. I can do that but I can't step into somebody's world and fight it and make that happen. Students tell me this too, "now that I see the world differently, now that I've studied these theories. I'm noticing when this has happened or that's happened. I'll see things through the guilt redemption cycle of Kenneth Burk. I'm starting to see that. I'm seeing those things and other people don't see them." Then, I ask them, "what's the value in it if you don't step in?" The answer comes down to: I make better communication choices because I see these things. While I can't change the world out there, I can make better communication choices in my world that will enhance the relationships between myself and someone else even though I want to change the world still.

Carol Thompson's thinking brings back to my mind the words of Jiddu Krishnamurti (1992), who said,

> All you can do is to alter your relationship with the world, not the world of Europe or America, but the world of your wife, your husband, your work, your home. There you can bring change, and that change moves in wider and wider circles. (p. 22)

The participants in this study were stars in various areas of study: from rhetoric to mass media. But they all could see the communication problems, the missed opportunities and choices that people have. They saw the absence of what could be as they believed in the possibilities of human communication. Karen Foss, for example, said:

> I just think that people do not think about communication choices and I think that we as communication professionals do. We understand the right choices. Not only do we know our choices, we know that we can construct the choices, that the choices are almost infinite. I am usually more interested in what are the possibilities being even in an oppressive encounter because there's always possibilities.

Tom Socha's comments aligned well with Karen's comments. He shared this point with me:

> So I think when I look at kids, especially, I see tremendous potentialities but I also see the discursive world around them is often time causing damage, harmful, it is not going to help them with their potentialities. And I want to twist that around. I want to change that.

In everyday interaction, the participants could see the actuality of how people communicated—the problems, the troubles, the utterances that hurt and damage, and all too often, they could also see what could have been, what should be. In her interview, Sandra Petronio, who has been active in translating research into practice, said "[I] look and think about how things can be better instead of how they are limiting." The difference between what people do and what they could do was particularly well-expressed in this moment with Larry Frey, who explained:

> For example, every question that people ask is a statement, but they don't phrase it as a statement. You know they don't say, "I see you as this," and "I'm wondering, you know, the reasons for why you engage in that behavior." They're making a statement, but they're saying, "why do you do that?" without putting the statement out there. And so I teach a course in which I teach people to recognize and to change all of their questions into statements. In fact, I don't allow them to ask any questions of others. They have to make statements of the people in the room. And I think that a lot of things like that we could point to and say, here is advice that would be given, like for example, you should always foreground the caring of the relationship before ever confronting somebody about what that person is doing. So rather than saying "I don't like that you do that," which is a statement and expresses the intent, it would be far better to say "Look, I am concerned, I care about you deeply, I'm concerned about our relationship, and I need to confront you about something, would that be okay?" Something like that.

For every moment of human interaction, there is what people are doing, and there is what people could be doing. There is reality and potentiality. Communication scholars see missed opportunities in many interactions, whether those are in interpersonal, family, organizational, or social contexts. The disciplinary gaze is fixed on the problems—what people are doing wrong. And it sees how communication could be better. At the same time, communication scholars rarely spoke of seeing successes in action, of seeing beauty in the moment, or connection. In that sense, our gaze sees possibilities, but that is not its daily purpose. We are looking for missed opportunities, not ones that have been accomplished. To quote Em Griffin, then, "let's find a point a contact" and "our world will be better place."

To summarize, the participants in this study saw human communication as a process of co-creation. They saw how participants' small, and taken-for-granted, behaviors, both verbal and nonverbal, created social reality. They noticed the patterns under construction, the multiple functions of messages, and the consequences of people's choices. With their disciplinary gaze, they experienced human communication differently than most people and longed for social change.

Conclusion

Communication scholars see and hear the details of human interaction. They see the microscopic performance of nonverbal actions. They notice people learning toward one another or moving away in space. They see the way parents extend their gaze to discipline their child. They notice tactile behaviors—where the touch is occurring, its strength, and intensity. They also hear the details of speech acts; they hear the complexities of messages, their design, but also their function. What are people doing with their talk? Is this message confirming or disconfirming? Is it a face-threat or an act of saving face? These are the questions of their inner voice. Finally, they see the missed moments of connection, the failures, and the ways in which people could be communicating more wisely. The fact is that communication scholars see and hear the details of human communication. They are, to quote Karen Foss, more "aware than the average person."

Most people, however, have not studied communication. As a result, they may not see, or be aware of, the complexities of human interaction. They cannot see face-threats, but they can feel the sting. They may not see the pupils dilating during a flirting moment, but they may feel the attraction that is taking place. They may not know the difference between a disconfirming message and a confirming one, or even how to design a message to move it in a more productive direction. The problem of communicating well, then, may have less to do with desire or want, and more to do with the inability to see or hear the poetics of communication. As Raymie McKerrow explained,

> the only difference between me and the other students in the classroom in terms of intelligence is my own experience…it is not that you can't see those things, but rather I have had more time to experience…you have to be open to those possibilities that you are not the only one seeing things that others do not see.

Or, said differently, the only difference between expert and non-expert are the coding schemes that inform their professional vision.

Scholars and teachers need to remember that learning about communication is not just a cognitive experience. Learning new concepts and theories also shapes what people see and informs the development of a professional vision. That is exactly what makes the vocabulary of the communication discipline so critical. Once people know the difference between confirming and disconfirming communication, they can see it in others or themselves. If people can see how communication unfolds, then they can make better choices and try new things, which is exactly what I did with my newly acquired knowledge of Northern Cardinals.

On a beautiful Sunday morning, my wife, Meg, and the kids, John Luke and Hugo and I took a morning walk. As we were talking, I captured in the corner of my eye, above in the trees, a quick movement. I looked up and saw a gray-ish, purple-ish bird. Immediately, I collected the family's attention, pointed, and lowered my voice: "Look, guys, this is a female Northern Cardinal." I couldn't help myself to make the call: "Whoit, whoit, whoit, purdy, purdy, purdy." The bird moved closer to us. With excitement, I said, "look, she is moving towards us." And then she sang to us and responded to my call. And that's when my wife drew her line: "Could you please stop flirting with the birds?"

References

Adelman, M. B., & Frey, L. R. (1997). *The fragile community: Living together with AIDS*. Mahwah, NJ: Lawrence Erlbaum.

Birdwhistell, R. L. (1970). Masculinity and femininity as display. In *Kinesics and context: Essays on body motion* (pp. 39–46). Philadelphia, PA: University of Pennsylvania Press.

Cody, M. J., & O'Hair, H. D. (1983). Nonverbal communication and deception: Differences in deception cues due to gender and communicator dominance. *Communications Monographs*, 50(3), 175–192.

Dreyfus, H. L., & Rabinow, P. (1982). *Michel Foucault: Beyond structuralism and hermeneutics*. Chicago, IL: University of Chicago Press.

Goodwin, C. (1994). Professional vision. *American Anthropologist*, 96(3), 606–633.

Knapp, M., Hall, J., & Horgan, T. (2013). Nonverbal communication in human interaction. Boston, MA: Wadsworth Cengage Learning.

Krishnamurti, J. (1992). *On relationship*. New York, NY: HarperCollins.

Nussbaum, J. F., Federowicz, M., & Nussbaum, P. D. (2009). *Brain health and optimal engagement in older adulthood*. Girona, Spain: Editorial Aresta.

Nussbaum, J. F., Miller-Day, M., & Fisher, C. (2009). *Communication and intimacy in older adulthood*. Girona, Spain: Editoria Aresta.

Pearce, W. B., & Pearce, K. A. (2000). Extending the theory of the coordinated management of meaning (CMM) through a community dialogue process. *Communication Theory*, 10(4), 405–423.

Socha, T. J., & Beck, G. A. (2015). Positive communication and human needs: A review and proposed organizing conceptual framework. *Review of Communication*, 15(3), 173–199.

Streeck, J., & Mehus, S. (2005). Microethnography: The study of practices. In K. Fitch & R. Sanders (Eds.), *Handbook of language and social interaction*. Mahwah, NJ: Lawrence Erlbaum.

Streeck, J., Goodwin, C., & LeBaron, C. (Eds.). (2011). *Embodied interaction: Language and body in the material world*. Cambridge, MA: Cambridge University Press.

Tracy, K., & Tracy, S. J. (1998). Rudeness at 911: Reconceptualizing face and face attack. *Human Communication Research*, 25(2), 225–251.

· 7 ·

HOW DO COMMUNICATION PROFESSORS COMMUNICATE ACROSS THEIR CAREER?

When I interviewed Wendy Leeds-Hurwitz, she was in Australia. At the end of my interview, I asked her to reflect on her journey. She said, "you know I was thinking about this before we started our conversation. We have been doing a lot of hiking in what they call the bush here. I found myself taking pictures of a tree trunk [and] you can see the rings." She explained to me, "you can see how old it is and which years, you know the thicker the rings mean it was a good year, there was a lot of rain and sod and the thin years are the years that there wasn't as much."

For Wendy, that tree trunk represented her own lifespan. She laughed, "the tree is not dead you know," but now "it feels a little bit like I am getting to see the attrition of the rings and the development of the rings, but I am also getting to shape the next rings." Much like a tree, human development is slow. As I will show in this chapter, this is particularly true for the ways in which communication professors grew in their approach to interaction.

The next two chapters answer one big question: how do communication professors communicate with others? This chapter, however, explores how their approach to communication developed across their career. What directions did they take? In what ways have they improved? How do they approach interaction now that is different from their past? Keep in mind that the participants we interviewed are some of the leading scholars in our field; all of them have taught communication courses for over 25 years. They have studied human interaction *in situ* or conducted experiments. They are social scientists, rhetoricians, ethnographers, or quantitative researchers. But, at the end of the day, they have to communicate with others too. They are professors, and spouses, brothers and sisters, or mothers and fathers. With these experiences, this chapter highlights that our participants moved away from themselves and toward others. Specifically, the participants in this study grew in four major directions. They moved, like the rings of a tree trunk, outward. First, they moved toward mindfulness. Second, they moved toward gentleness and learned to be increasingly more considerate about the implications of language on others. Third, they moved toward deeper listening, thereby giving more space for others to express themselves. Fourth, they moved toward playfulness, seeing opportunities in everyday interaction for play and humor. Unlike the tree trunk Wendy spoke about, though, their communication skills did not weaken. They strengthened in the direction of others with humility.

A Movement Toward Mindfulness

Earlier in the book, I described how communication scholars are hypersensitive to interaction. In a full chapter, we also explored the ways communication scholars see the world around them. But, many of the scholars I interviewed were relatively self-conscious about their own communication and about their own challenges in interacting with others. In other words, the participants in this study recognized their efforts at trying to communicate better while also recognizing their own limitations. Communicating well is not easy—it cannot be done perfectly. It is complex, fraught with challenges, and even though we have, as Stephen Littlejohn explained, "limitless options," we often fall short. Being able to express these complexities is indeed a growth in one's thinking and a competency. In this section, I show how communication scholars moved in the direction of greater communication competency by becoming more reflective, understanding, and humble.

It might be helpful to consider the interviews in light of a popular model about how people learn and grow. Learning, some scholars have shown, involves moving from unconsciousness to consciousness, and then back to unconsciousness (see Howell, 1982). In learning a new art such as communication, *unconscious incompetence* is the beginning place. At this stage, the individual is not aware of their own communication and their shortcomings. They may, for instance, overestimate their ability to listen to another person or not know at all if they criticize or compliment more frequently.

In the second and third level, the learner undergoes an important transformation. The second level is *conscious incompetence*. At this stage, the person may "become aware that something is amiss but they may not know what to do" (Morell, Sharp, & Crandall, 2002, p. 532). The third level is *conscious competence*. Having learned specific techniques, concepts, or skills, the individual is now able to consciously apply what they have learned. A person may learn, for instance, that an effective technique to provide feedback is to start with a strength, describe an area of improvement, and end with a positive summary. With this technique in mind, the individual can then consciously provide feedback effectively. According to Howell (1982), "the third level adds understanding. Understanding is knowing what you do and why it works or does not work" (p. 532).

The fourth level is *unconscious competence*. Here, the individual can "effectively modify their behavior without reflecting on how they are doing it" (Morell, Sharp, & Crandall, 2002, p. 5). They are communicating with skill and technique without doing it consciously—it is simply a natural part of how they engage in that process.

Moving from unconscious incompetence to unconscious competence offers an important framework for reflecting about how to build expertise. It is helpful for thinking about a single skill or a set of techniques, but because the art of communication is complex, challenging, and dilemmatic, unconscious competence is not a stage many of our participants claimed for themselves. In fact, most participants in the study positioned themselves "in between" the second and third stage, recognizing both their incompetence and the fact that they were getting better.

My interview with Dan O'Hair best exemplifies what I am trying to express. I asked him: As you know, communication is something we study and that we can research. But it is also something that we cannot escape from; we have to engage in communication every day. What realizations have you had throughout your development about your own communication? This is what he said:

It is two things and they sound contradictory. I am probably more disappointed the longer I live in my ability to communicate, yet at the same time I know that I have never been better. And so in some way it is kind of frustrating for me. I fully understand that I do not have the vocabulary pallet that a lot of my colleagues do. I have a very thick Texas accent that is noticeable by a lot of people. I always wish that I had a brain that could increase its capacity to analyze what someone has said much, much, much faster so that I could do a more complicated analysis before I actually open my mouth to respond.

A few seconds later, Dan repeated the key statement: "The older I get, the more disappointed I get in myself while at the same time realizing that I am probably better than I have ever been." As we'll see below, the participants I interviewed saw themselves as improving, but they also acknowledged their shortcomings. Dan's statement cues a certain degree of awareness and consciousness.

Em Griffin echoed some of Dan O'Hair's point: a constant attention to what one is doing or saying, its possible implications on others, or the consequences that would emerge. After I asked a few similar questions, Em Griffin did get a little frustrated with me, but in that frustration came a meaningful answer. As he explained:

> If I sound a little bit frustrated, Julien, you've asked this question a few different ways and I mean, *I'm thinking about it all the time*. It's not like, "Oh gee, I thought of something last month, and I wonder how I'm coming across, or I wonder why this happened." It's part of my DNA.

Predominantly, the communication scholars I interviewed thought about communication a lot. When they interacted with others, they analyzed it as it was happening, sorting through the potential responses. When I interviewed Betsy Bach, who has been a faculty member at the University of Montana since 1984, she expressed the sentiment that her consciousness about communication could not be stopped. She said, "Well, it's just like 'Oh my god! Can I just listen to a conversation without, you know, trying to figure out communicatively what is going on and what's behind the words?'" Analysis of interaction *in situ* was common among participants. It was both a way to be mindful, to be attentive, but also a distraction.

More importantly, perhaps, is the realization of one's limitations as a communicator, of what one person can do while attending to many complexities that occur moment-by-moment, turn-of-talk by turn-of talk. The realization of the difference between what one wants to do and what one does or between knowing what to do and not doing it. That is wisdom. This tension was well expressed in my interview with Lynn Turner:

I can tell you what I think, *I don't always succeed in doing this*, but I certainly am very aware of how to be empathic, and how to maybe take a pause and not say the first thing coming into my head, and to use "I messages" and … to offer positive comments and try to go in the 5 to 1 ratio. You know, 5 good things for every 1 negative thing. …I'm definitely mindful but *I don't always succeed*.

It was also expressed in my interview with Raymie McKerrow, who wrote 15 textbooks on effective public communication, when he said, "I fail more than I succeed in terms of satisfying myself as a communicator." He added, "I think I am my worst own critic in other words…so there is a humility that I think probably defines my approach to all communication." As he reflected, he made his point more acute:

But it is that sense of constantly being aware of the imperfection of how communication functions. It is not a perfect system and what you think people are hearing may or may not be what they are hearing. And you have to constantly be aware of the fact that as clear as you may want to be, you may not be as clear as you think.

The limitations and difficulties of communicating well were exposed consistently throughout the interviews. Communication scholars described that they were getting better but that they were not immune to incompetency. Steven Beebe explained, "I pay attention to when things aren't going well. I stop and say 'OK, what am I doing wrong here?' And often what I find is, on reflection, I'll see things that I didn't see in the moment." As evidenced in this excerpt, Steven was conscious of both what he could do and what he could not do. He said, "some of the skills we teach are very rational. So in my own communication, I'm not immune from having conflict. I'm not immune from poor listening." At the same time, Steven nevertheless noted that he has resources on his side. He explained: "I have some tools, just like, the plumbers have leaks, but a plumber has tools to go address those leaks." He concluded by saying: "My communication still leaks…I am not the perfect communicator that I aspire to be…but I have some resources."

Jon Nussbaum echoed a similar point by reflecting on the humility it takes to see one's own incompetence. He said,

another thing is you have to understand your own incompetence, you know, be humble. If you have this awareness of your own incompetence, you can give the other person a break, and you can listen to what they're saying and try to slow things down. Viewed from this perspective, moving toward conscious incompetence is thus a critical development and a way to build empathy about the challenge of interacting well, and it naturally teaches humility.

At the end of his thought, he emphasized this point: "it takes practice. All of us are not competent communicators. We are just not."

Being able to understand features of one's own communication and being able to see new possibilities is at the heart of increasing consciousness. Lynn Turner's comments aligned well with Jon Nussbaum's perspective. She pointed it out: "Just because you understand it does not necessarily mean you are going to be able to do it differently." Another challenge that shaped competency is that interaction involves more than a single person. She said, "the other thing with communication [that is] captivating but frustrating is that you can only control you. You can't control what another person does." "However," she explained, "you can understand it so that if we explain something about those unwanted repetitive conflict patterns, we might still slide into them, but now you can see, 'that's why. That was the trigger.'" Understanding our triggers, if you will, is a lifelong journey taught both by experience and communication theory, and a part of building communication competency.

The inner tension for many communication scholars was to balance their sense of incompetence with their attempt to be competent—to act differently in spite of the triggers that could move them in an unwanted direction. In my interview with Gerry Philipsen, he spoke of this inner tension, and once again, the realization of personal progress toward competency and the natural disappointment of falling short. He said:

> I internalize deeply the disposition to refute, to challenge, and I think I have gotten over that to a certain extent and that's not something that I can totally get over with. I think I am frequently looking for the weakness, looking for something to rebut, and so I say to myself, "don't do that."…I am joking about this very serious point with me because I feel that much of what I know how to do, it is not necessarily how I want to be in the world.

There are too many turns of talk, too many nonverbal and verbal cues, to make the right move every time. Communicating well is a challenge, and even though participants felt that they grew as communicators, they consistently expressed their own failures. John Daly, in particular, warned of the difference between being a good analyst of communication practices and a good communicator. "Just because you're a good analyst doesn't mean you're good at it," he said. "I think I'm a much better advisor about communication than I am a good communicator myself …. I'm not sure it's a requirement for you to be a good communicator necessarily to teach the stuff." Yet, at the end of this reflection, he revealed that he thought quite deeply about his own communication. "I probably lose more sleep than most people do over my communication," he told me. "I ask myself, 'why did I say that? What did I mean? How could I have said that differently?'" There is, as John expressed, a difference between analyzing communication and engaging in it well. And yet, in the middle of the night, he is thinking to himself, "How could I have said that differently?" a question that would begin to make a difference in everyday interaction.

Larry Frey's reflections expressed a similar concern. "It's not unusual," he said, "that people who teach something can't necessarily do it all that well." He added, "You can teach art without having to be a great artist, or you can teach film without having to make films." But, as he finished that thought, he expressed a significant difference between these contexts and the field of human communication. "It can't help but come into my personal life." Notice in the following example, how Larry's comment speaks to the tension of realizing progress in one's ability to communicate, the recognition of both success and failure, and the life-long journey of making progress:

> In terms of personal relationships, say with my wife, again, I'm vulnerable in the same way others are, in that I get caught up in patterns that I know at the time I don't really want to be in. And over the course of time, I've tried to develop strategies to get out of those patterns, and sometimes I'm successful, sometimes I'm not. So, it's not that we can't practice what we preach, it's just that it's a lot harder. And we, like everybody else, often don't succeed as well as we might. So I think it's different to be a helper than it is to be the helpee, just as it is different to be a teacher than it is to be a student. Doesn't mean they don't blend together at times and the skills can't work, but it means there's a place and time for particular things, particular ways of being with regard to communicating. Not all of the time can I call on those skills in all of those situations that I'd like to. So yeah, sometimes I might yell at somebody, but I know that's not an effective strategy, or an effective behavior for accomplishing what I want to accomplish. I think I am pretty quick at recognizing that, quicker now after studying it than I was before studying it. So I could go days in a relationship, let's say, being pretty angry with somebody, and that doesn't happen anymore. It might last an hour, half an hour or something. So I have improved over the course of time on those problematic communication behaviors.

The professors I interviewed consistently expressed a great sense of consciousness about how to communicate well with others. They marked, as we will see below, that they became better communicators throughout their lifespan. Robert Craig, for example, said, "I'm sure all of these years of being a communication professional have made me a better communicator." Similarly, Larry Frey said, "I am far clearer today." He explained, if you look at, say, expressing affection and arguing with people, or having other difficulties, each of those in a way I have become far better [at] dealing with the interaction and to have faith and trust that the communication will massage it.

At the same time, they were consistently disappointed by their capacity. They were aware of the potentiality of what should be, but brought back to reality with what is.

In his book on the great virtues, the philosopher Comte-Sponville (2001) began the book by recognizing the challenge of writing about virtues. "To venture to write about the virtues," he wrote, "is to subject one's self-esteem to constant bruising, to be made acutely aware, again and again, of one's own mediocrity" (p. 5). "To think about the virtues," he emphasized, "is to take measure of the distance separating us from them. To think about their excellence is to think about our own inadequacies or wretchedness" (p. 5). In the end, I think that is what these great scholars were communicating: they are self-conscious about communication, constantly thinking about what it could be and what it is not, what they have done and what they could have done, and in this process, are constantly bruised by their own limitations and imperfections.

A Movement Toward Gentleness

In a story shared by my colleague Avinash Thombre, a family is eating dinner together. Everything is on the table and all they are missing is some toast. The mother places the bread in the toaster and burns almost every single piece. Her mind is elsewhere and she places the pieces of toast on the table. The father picks one up, puts some butter on it, and eats it, even though it is terribly burnt. His little girl sees this unfolding and can't believe that her father is not saying anything about the fact that the toast is burnt. "They're completely black," she thinks to herself. But her father is eating the toast eagerly. The girl doesn't say anything, but she can't help but think about this event. At night, as her father is tucking her in, she asks him: "Why didn't you tell mom that the toast was burned and why did you eat one?" He said, "you know, your mom has worked hard all day. She has come home to take care of you and me. She has cooked a wonderful dinner for us." He added, "Burned toast is not going to hurt anyone. I don't need to hurt your mom's feelings after everything she has done all day."

Being gentle is at the heart of communicating well. In his work, Comte-Sponville (2001) explained that "gentleness is, to begin with, a kind of peace, either real or desired: It is the opposite of war, cruelty, brutality, aggressiveness, violence" (p. 186). Said more positively, "Gentleness is a strength, which is what makes it a virtue; it is strength in a state of peace, serene and gentle, full of patience and leniency" (p. 186). In my interviews with participants, I found a consistent movement toward gentleness in the way they reported communicating. Participants grew more and more gentle with others, with their word choices, and, in some instances, with themselves. This lifelong movement spanned across their careers and unfolded in many ways.

Take, for instance, Karen Foss, who, at one point in the interview, shared, "I had a huge 'aha' moment when I realized that I was a feminist bully and I needed to stop doing that." With such a powerful statement, I asked her to expand. This is what she said:

> Well it relates to both, everyday things and how I relate to people in the field. I mean, I came into the field from the Women's Movement and I wanted things to be a particular way, you know, I wanted the world to change so it was better for women. I didn't want women to change their names when they got married....I wanted the Equal Rights Amendment passed and then I thought of, you know, as part of this question of persuasion, I thought, well, "How are you any different? You know, you have this cause that you are trying to cram down people's throats and what difference does it make to you whether they become feminist or not? Or whether they change their names? So just stop it Foss! [Laughs] Let them live their lives like you want to be able to live your life." So now I think I am much better in the classroom and with graduate students at not saying, "Well, it's got to be this way." You know it does not have to be that way! [Laughs] It can be lots of ways and that's one of the interesting things about the world, it's that we don't all think the same way and if we all did we would be bored to tears, you know? So that was kind of another revelation that maybe I was just as bad as the people I was critiquing [laughs].

From this moment on, Karen tried to become more gentle in her approach to conversation and argumentation. She approached it with more openness, with less confrontation, and with less assumptions about who is right and who is wrong. She moved toward what Sonja Foss named invitational rhetoric, "an invitation to understanding as a means to create a relationship rooted in equality, immanent value, and self-determination" (Foss & Griffin, 1995, p. 5). As she became more open, she approached conversations very differently:

I don't try to persuade people nearly as much as I used to about anything. So if I have a strong opinion, I may say, "Have you thought about this?" Or I'll say "Oh interesting! I look at it from this angle." So I add to the conversation but I do not insist to adapt that view. Because I think I am also interested in having as many perspectives get into the conversation, to lay it on the table. Because then I think we have more to choose from, more to draw from. We just have more options.

Karen Foss simply became more gentle in her approach to conversation. For Kristine Muñoz, it was about becoming less intimidating. She said, "I am more gentle with people than I used to be. I am more aware of my ability to intimidate and hurt people so I try hard not to." Earlier in the interview, she explained that when she communicates with people, she pays attention to whether she is frightening them. She said:

I say frightening them because I hear so often and in so many contexts and in so many ways that people are intimidated by me, and much as I say I think that's more about them than it is about me, the reality is, if somebody is intimated by me that is unpleasant for them. And most of the time, 99% of the time, I don't want that to be, so I try to make that not happen. Once every 2 or 3 years, it is OK with me....If there is a butt that needs kicking and I am just the person to do it, but the rest of the time that is not a good thing. So I try to be sensitive to whether that's happening and what I can do to minimize it.

Kristine, like Karen, slowly grew more gentle and approached conversations with an intentional awareness about the possible consequences. Their own communication, they realized, affected people. In my interview with John Daly, he echoed this point by emphasizing that we have to be careful with each other:

I'm more careful now than I used to be. I'm less sure than I used to be about many things, and less direct about some things. I'm not sure if that's me because of the communication field, or me as an adult, and those are confounding variables. I wish I had a better way of putting it, but I think it's just—it may be age as much as anything else.

It is true that one dominant variable is age—and scholars spoke to this. This project cannot identify the variable that makes the difference, but it can note the consistent movement toward gentleness. For communication professors, the impetus to be gentle lies in core principles: communication is irreversible and it affects others. In one instance, for example, Carol Thompson said that everyday communicators "need to recognize that what you do and say has an effect on people." She came to this realization with the work of Gibb (1961) on supportive and defensive climates as well as her ability to affect students positively on their work:

> [W]hen you work with people you tend to be disconfirming a lot of times…like one time, to get through school, I was a secretary in the summer and my boss would come and say, "this is the worst typing I've ever seen, oh yes," and throw the paper down and say there are two errors on that page. So this is what you learn to do early on, so your tendency is to do that again. Like you tend to parent the way you were parented. You learn that and so you learn some of these negative behaviors. So it was a real "aha" moment for me to learn about some of these other ways of doing it and then catching myself. I mean, even writing on student papers. "This is tangent and dull," you know, which actually appeared on one of the papers I got from one of my professors, "your spade writing is OK but the rest is tangent and dull." How evaluative is that? It was an aha moment to realize what an effect that has on other people that you can instead say, "generally the piece tends to work really well. There's a problem in this paragraph and so and so on and when you fix those you will have a quality piece of work," which is quite different than saying "the work is good but the writing is tangent and dull," and so that was turning point when I realized the power of being non evaluative. It is really powerful.

In her book *Making Contact*, the world-renown family counselor Virgina Satir (1976) wrote, "Making real contact means that we make ourselves responsible for what comes out of us. Anything that injures self-esteem reduces the opportunity to make good contact." Throughout the interviews, the ways in which communication professors talked about their growth cued that they slowly realized Satir's message. They incrementally paid attention to the ways in which communication is irreversible and consequential. Steven Littlejohn, for example, framed it as a personal guiding question: "How can I respond in a way that helps us move away from harm and towards value?" He said, "So thinking about it that way, or 'What can I do right now that would be the right thing to do?'" He explained it more deeply:

> So, for example, put defensiveness, it is one that is going to move you more toward harm and away from value. To hold off defensiveness, to see if you can just take a few minutes to acknowledge what the other person is trying to say, to understand a little bit better where they are coming from, you are a little closer to value and a little bit further away from harm.

Gentleness is inherently nonviolent. In communication, it involves making choices that move toward adding value rather than creating harm. It is the realization that our communication affects others. Robert Craig, for example, put it this way. He said, "I need to be aware of the effect I am having on people." Similarly, Carol Thompson explained it from her personal experience: it was the realization that "what you do and say has an effect on the people with whom you are working. Another way of saying it is it has consequences…. So you've got to pay attention to that." The communication professors I interviewed became slowly and increasingly more gentle. They realized the foundational principle of human interaction: it is consequential and it affects others. Virtues are rarely attainable. They are simply guides for action that call us toward excellence (see Aristotle, 2004). Communication professors, thus, were not inherently gentle—they moved in that direction, increasingly becoming more mindful and attentive to others. Which is also what led them to listen more closely.

A Movement Toward Deeper Listening

For many communication scholars, listening is "*the* quintessential positive interpersonal communication behavior as it connotes an appreciation of and an interest in the other" (Bodie, 2012, p. 109). Listening is the critical component of dialogic communication (e.g., Cissna & Anderson, 1998; 2004) and what some scholars call interpersonal transcendence, a moment of interaction in which "participants experience a sense of discovery, creation, and a feeling of connection, or 'sharedness,' that could only be achieved via interaction" (Greene & Herbers, 2011, p. 66). Across the 30 interviews we conducted, the act of listening was treated as paramount. Most, if not all, participants spoke about the importance of listening. In fact, excerpts we collected from all interviews on listening exceeded 36 pages of text. With this in mind, this section suggests that faculty members increasingly moved in the direction of listening more deeply. In general terms, they started by speaking well and ended up with listening.

In my interview with Dan O'Hair, I reflected on a previous comment and asked him, "with that in light, what changes would you say you have made to the way you interact with other people?" Dan took a pause. "I have," and then he hesitated. "I do not know whether this is the case or not. I have made a conscious effort to listen more." And, of course, he immediately pointed out the challenge of measuring improvement. He said, "I think that anyone who says 'oh I listen more,' that seems a little bit arrogant, you do not know if you are or not … but I have made a conscious effort to do that and to be more open to individuals." Lynn Turner, our professor from Marquette University, realized that she liked talking more than listening. "So I have to work on that," she said in the interview. "I think that is kind of an occupational hazard," she continued. "I think when people do like to talk, going into a field like being a professor is a great choice, but listening, of course, is extremely important. So I try to work on that."

Many communication professors reported that listening was not their natural impulse. It was a direction that required effort, attention, and discipline. Michael Kleine, for example, described it as a want—a desire to listen and an active goal in human interaction. He said, "I want to listen. I want to respect positions that are different from mine." Listening is not easily done. It is an action to be desired rather than one that is taken for granted. Later on, he explained this point even more with Kristina Godfrey, who conducted the interview. He said:

> Even as we talk right now, I am trying to see you as a subject not an object. I think that it sounds so simple, but it's difficult. You really have to work on understanding that those we communicate with are human beings. So I find myself in conversations asking questions more than just talking. I know I'm monopolizing this conversation, I try and avoid that. I think monopolizing conversations is a common art and difficult to deal with. But dialogue is everything.

Listening well is a challenge. But many of our communication professors had the theoretical knowledge to do it well. Throughout the interviews, they described their understanding of the science and art of listening. Lynn Turner again said, listening "doesn't mean just being quiet." It means "focusing on the other person and being other-oriented, and not being so concerned about getting your own ideas out there [and] being a little bit more relationally attuned." Arthur Bochner expressed it well too. Listening, he said, "is an openness to the other." It is "trying to recognize how the other person is thinking [and] how they are feeling. It means "being with" another person. "Most of the time," he ended, "we don't understand each other."

Most communication professionals saw listening as the most important goal of their communication. Tom Socha, for example, explained his approach to interaction. He said, "The first thing I pay attention to is I want to make certain that I hear them; that they are heard. Every single interaction," he added, "I absolutely want to make certain that they feel heard." Em Griffin, similarly, exclaimed: "I do hopefully more listening than talking." Steven Beebe said, "it's more important to listen than speak." Communication is all about "being other-centered, audience-centered, and needs-centered." The point is that our participants spoke of the value of listening and moved in its direction. They incrementally paid attention to the details of how to engage with others with a listening focus. Consider, as a final example, how Stephen Littlejohn prepares for an interaction with a student:

> I have a student who is coming to see me and talk to me about something conceptual and I know that it is going to be difficult. I would put myself in that mode, "OK, do not be quick to respond, kind of set aside your hard feelings about the subject. And instead just ask them the questions, try to be open-minded, see if you can acknowledge their point of view, see if you can make them feel heard, and then state my point of view." I can put myself in that mode by thinking ahead of time, not just walk into it.

Listening deeply to others is a lifelong effort. The interviews reveal that communication professors moved from speaking well to listening well. They became more focused on the other, on giving voice, and on solving interpersonal problems by getting to know the other's perspective. Betsy Bach, in fact, said that one big change she experienced in her growth is "knowing that I don't always have to be the talker." She had learned the skill of moving in the direction of others, and to say, over and over again: "let's hear what you think."

A Movement Toward Playfulness

I'm driving in the city with my wife next to me. We are up on Hillcrest, a small historic neighborhood carved into a forest that is centrally located between downtown Little Rock and West Little Rock. We reach Allsop Park and take a left down a windy road toward the river. It's covered by the trees, with long shadows, and there is a significant drop of temperature, as the trees protect this road from the heat of summer. We're talking and goofing around, making puns and being witty. In one moment, I ask her: "OK, who am I more like, Batman or Spiderman?" "Oh baby," she says, "you're more like Green Lantern." My heart sinks a little, but I appreciate the witty comment and we laugh together the whole way down.

One of the wonders of human communication is that language can be used not just to share information, but to create humor, to laugh, and to play. Although not everyone talked about the importance of playfulness in communication, many scholars I interviewed noted its importance, found themselves playing in the course of interaction, and seized the moment to engage, make contact, and create laughter. They found opportunities to be playful, to redirect the conversation, to move it into uncharted territories, or simply to have fun. This idea was well-exemplified in my interview with Gerry Philipsen, who said:

> I also, and maybe to my discredit, I am also listening for little fun moments, little openings and some people close to me refer to it or say that I tease them a lot, that I play, and I am always looking for opportunities for play and sometimes that does not serve me well. And I have to kind of check that and I realize that sometimes it just gets to the point to where it is dysfunctional for me and not pleasing to other people.

Notice here that Gerry is looking for "openings" for "opportunities for play." He is curious about where the interaction might go. His approach is unconventional, but learning about human communication lends itself well to playfulness. Arvind Singhal expressed an identifiable approach and narrated his ways of being playful with more depth. Consider here what he said:

> And you can ask my two boys they sometimes feel very embarrassed about what their dad is going to do because I am not shy of saying things which you would not expect a person to say to a stranger or to a non-stranger. So for instance, if I am at the counter and they are behind me and I am ordering say my ice cream so I would say something like, "Oh yeah, I'd like the pistachio" and then I might say something like "and I'll take it with some masala." OK, now you know this is going to completely throw them off. Masala is an Indian term for spice and they have absolutely no clue and this is going to engender a reaction like "masala what's masala?" and you know my boys are like, "ugh, God!" you know and of course I am being playful and creative and joyful because of how they handle that response. It is very revealing to me as a playful person, and most of the time I trust the process and the conversation ends up at a very different place than where it began.

Many communication professionals spoke about the significance of humor and play in their lives. Dan O'Hair, as another example, aligned very much with Gerry and Arvind. In the interview, I asked him about how he communicates with people in his life. "I have always been a huge fan of humor," he said. "I have wanted to be funny all my life, and I wanted to be 'fun-nier' all my life." He added that "it takes a lot of intelligence to be really good at using humor." But observe the way his next comment aligns even more with the interviews that I quoted above:

> And I sort of, like, regardless of the context, I have always looked for the opportunity to be funny or have fun while I was in that context. And my family has been extremely supportive in that way. And I guess my colleagues have as well because I seem to be trying it more often than I used to.

Dan O'Hair's comment is important here: "I have always looked for the opportunity to be funny or have fun." Across the interviews, communication scholars saw human interaction as a series of opportunities; as moves that could be made or not made. Being funny or playful could be part of any interaction if one only looked at interaction as a series of opportunities.

For many, the opportunity to be playful and to use humor unfolded in the sphere of the classroom. Being a good teacher involves lots of communication skills, but using humor is a key way to relate to students. Jon Nussbaum learned this when he asked himself: "What did the good teachers do that the bad teachers didn't do?" His own finding was: "And it seemed to be that the good teachers had a much more engaging communicative style. They could tell good stories and they used humor." Raymie McKerrow alluded to a similar point: "One constant," he said about his teaching career, "is probably my satire." He explained further, "I use satire in the classroom. I have had students comment on the fact that I keep telling them I am not funny and they tell me that I am." Being humorous is a way to be playful with communication and communication professors exemplified it in their own lives—both inside and outside of the classroom.

Conclusion

This chapter explored core tendencies in communication professors' development in the way that they communicate with others. Communicating well is a lifelong journey and an art that cannot be mastered. Yet, as we saw in the interviews, participants grew in their consciousness about the way they interact, slowly became more gentle, moved from speaking to listening more, and became more free to play in interaction.

Communicating well is not easy. It is an art that requires practice, love, and maturity. Sometimes, as displayed in this story by Gerry Philipsen, a single moment can nudge us in a more productive direction. One morning, Gerry walked in his office. As always he settled down and then swung by his mailbox. He placed his hand inside and found a sealed letter addressed to him. He opened it and found an anonymous note:

"There are two kinds of people in this department. There are those who tear people down and those who build people up. You are the latter kind."

At first, Gerry shared, "I was glad. But then, I was ashamed." "Maybe," he thought at the time, "I could live my life by trying to live up to that. I could try to build people up." That moment created a ring of experience that strengthened his tree trunk.

References

Bodie, G. D. (2012). Listening as positive communication. In T. Socha & M. Pitts (Eds.), *The positive side of interpersonal communication* (pp. 109–125). New York, NY: Peter Lang Publishing.

Cissna, K. N., & Anderson, R. (1998). Theorizing about dialogic moments: The Buber-Rogers position and postmodern themes. *Communication Theory, 8*(1), 63–104.

Cissna, K. N., & Anderson, R. (2004). Public dialogue and intellectual history: Hearing multiple voices. In K. Anderson, L. A. Baxter, & K. Cissna (Eds.), *Dialogue: Theorizing difference in communication studies* (pp. 193–208). Thousand Oaks, CA: Sage.

Comte-Sponville, A. (2001). *A small treatise on the great virtues: The uses of philosophy in everyday life* (C. Temerson, Trans.). New York, NY: Henry Holt (Original work published 1996).

Foss, S. K., & Griffin, C. L. (1995). Beyond persuasion: A proposal for an invitational rhetoric. *Communications Monographs, 62*(1), 2–18.

Gibb, J. R. (1961). Defensive communication. *Journal of Communication, 11*(3), 141–148.

Greene, J. O., & Herbers, L. E. (2011). Conditions of interpersonal transcendence. *The International Journal of Listening, 25*(1–2), 66–84.

Howell, W. S. (1982). *The empathic communicator.* Belmont, CA: Wadsworth.

Morell, V. W., Sharp, P. C., & Crandall, S. J. (2002). Creating student awareness to improve cultural competence: Creating the critical incident. *Medical Teacher, 24*(5), 532–534.

Satir, V. (1976). *Making contact.* Ann Arbor, MI: University of Michigan Press.

· 8 ·

WHAT BEHAVIORS DO COMMUNICATION PROFESSORS VALUE?

I meet Arvind Singhal at the headquarters of Heifer International in Little Rock, Arkansas, where I live. He proposed this get-together because he was driving with his family from Texas to Ohio and offered to do the interview in person while they stopped to visit Little Rock. I arrive early, enter the cafeteria, and see Arvind already interacting with someone. When I approach, Arvind stands up, embraces me warmly, introduces me to his friend, and shares a few positive remarks about me and the project. The other person is ready to go and says good-bye. Arvind says, "I've got to do one more thing before we start. I have to text my family about where to meet at lunch." He grabs his phone, stares at the screen, and slows down the process of writing this message. In fact, he begins to talk to me about how to write this message—a simple note to his family about meeting him here for lunch rather than where they had planned to go. He says, "You've got to be careful about how to frame what you are asking. People don't like to be told what to do." Instead, he smiles, "a question might work better." I don't ask about the whole message, but he types in a question: "Why not meet here at the beautiful headquarters of Heifer International?" He keeps on typing, but interjects a few comments on the way about crafting this message. Most people would have written this small request in less than 5 seconds. But this message took him several minutes to design. Arvind Singhal's approach to this simple text, it turns out, is how many communication professionals engage in the act of communication.

In the previous chapter, we examined how participants' approach to human interaction grew throughout their lifespan. This chapter focuses on the behaviors they enact. We found that communication professionals we interviewed are aware of their own communication and its consequences, but their general approach to practicing communication is not directed. No one, for example, said: "when I communicate with others, I focus on six key behaviors that I try to practice." There was a keen interest in communicating more effectively, and many reported the effort of speaking well, but the direction was loose. Nevertheless, participants in one way or another reported engaging in specific communication behaviors. These behaviors were either valued, expressed directly or indirectly, or enacted in the interview itself. To reveal those behaviors, I draw on a model of positive communication I developed that is theoretically grounded and heuristic (see Mirivel, 2014). Using this model as a coding scheme, I discuss the significant communication behaviors that communication professors valued. The chapter proceeds by first introducing the model and then illustrating its components with examples from the interviews.

A Model of Positive Communication

Entering my capstone course at the University of Northern Iowa, I sat as usual around the C-shaped classroom. Marvin Jensen, my teacher and mentor, welcomed us warmly as we entered. This day was my last class as an undergraduate student. Mr. Jensen distributed a handout on which he had handwritten a proposition to the class. The document distinguished a person's profession from his or her job. A profession, he argued, is the core mission of your discipline. For example, "A physician's profession is to alleviate suffering," he wrote. "A person may have many jobs," but his profession may remain the same. The profession of a communication student, he suggested, is "to exemplify that the spoken word, spoken honorably and well, can make a difference that no other form of communication can equal."

In 2014, and with Mr. Jensen's words in mind, I developed a model of positive communication (Mirivel, 2014; see Figure 1). The model contributes to a larger conversation in the field that focuses on the positive side of communication (e.g., Socha & Beck, 2015; Socha & Pitts, 2012, 2013). As seen below, the model is a synthesis of communication behaviors (or speech acts) that generally function positively in human interaction—at work or at home. Those behaviors, I argue, produce high-quality relationships and cultivate positive climates. In addition to being descriptive, the model is also normative. It is a guide for everyday interaction and a call to practice positive communication. Consider its general principles and the speech acts that I recommend.

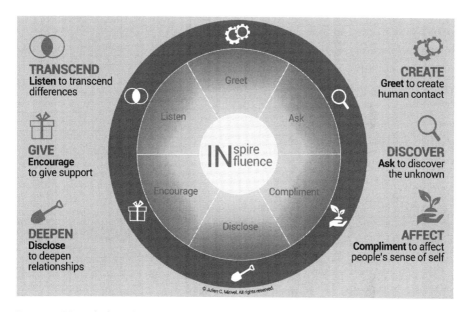

Figure 1. Mirivel's (2014) Model of Positive Communication.

Greet to Create Human Contact

The model begins with greetings. Greeting, I propose, creates human contact. From the work of Harvey Sacks (1992) to the Language in the Workplace Project in New Zealand (e.g., Holmes, 2003), researchers have shown that greeting sequences create the possibility of human contact and that their presence or absence is consequential. In the workplace, greetings can foster collegiality and good interpersonal relationships (see Holmes, 2000; Waldvogel, 2005). In education, the presence or absence of greetings from teachers affects students' performances on examinations and retention rates (e.g., Singhal, 2013). In medical interaction, greetings "set a positive tone for the encounter" and help to "develop a therapeutic clinical relationship" (Makoul,

Zick, & Green, 2007, p. 1174). At home, couples who have been married for at least 50 years cite greetings as one of the most important behaviors they enact (Young, 2004). Across contexts, research suggests that greeting others respectfully and warmly matters.

The communication professors we interviewed echoed the importance of greetings for human interaction and reflected on the significance of greetings. Allan Ward from the University of Arkansas at Little Rock, for example, said, "like greeting 'hello, how are you?' It doesn't mean people want a medical checkup on 'how are you.' It's saying, 'I am a human being, I recognize you are too.'" Similarly, Carol Thompson explained, "What you do and say is part of that co-construction of that relationship. You can't get away from it and it goes back to something as simple as how you say 'hi' to someone." She pressed on:

> Is it "hi"? What kind of relationship am I creating? Very bland and neutral. Or [is it] "hi, it's very good to see you!" You know and you move towards somebody. You're beginning to create a more positive relationship, simply by the way you say "hi."

Some scholars spoke of the importance of greetings directly. For others, it was mentioned in passing or as a point of reflection. For example, at the end of my conversation with John Peters, he pointed out that he can say thank you in about 30 languages and that he "can have long conversations in about six." "That builds intimacy," he told me. "Because it's something that you share with the other, it's that language." In almost all cultures that we know of, human interaction begins with greeting sequences. Learning to speak a new language begins by learning how to greet—or, more accurately, by learning to make contact.

For Arvind Singhal, making contact is crucial. There is something mystical about how the opening moments of meeting someone new can enact a sense of potentiality. Arvind explained this point to me. He said: "If I say 'hello' to my friend Julien and the quality of our interaction is good, that relationship will continue." His voice more focused now, he pushed this thought further: "You may meet somebody after 10 years. You may not remember what you may have talked about, but you would know exactly how it felt when you were with that person." "So," he said, "I think this notion of how it felt focuses on the quality of the interaction and that is not a small statement." Consider what he said next:

That is a rather big statement about the possibility that is invested in every micro second interaction you have with anybody professional, personal, or otherwise, because no matter what the outcome is, if the feeling was one which elevated you it creates the conditions for other interactions to happen down the line. It's not communication as a one-off micro-interaction that's closed in space or time, but it is evolving cascading energizing potentiality that you seed when you make that first encounter.

The first moment of human interaction, the greeting sequence, is packed with meaning and consequences. It is where relationships are created and managed.

During our conversation, John Daly reflected even more about the way to greet another person. "Most people," he said, "when they see people, they say 'nice to meet you.'" Maybe, there is a better way, he suggested. Especially if "you can't remember if you've met, instead say 'nice to see you.'" As he put it, "saying 'nice to see you' works just as well, but it doesn't run the risk of alienating anyone." The details, many communication professors expressed, matter.

In line with the model of positive communication, communication scholars directly or indirectly spoke to the significance of greetings. In the end, the model calls for an attentiveness to greetings and the courage to move in the direction of others. As Tom Socha shared with me, communication is an invitation: "when you greet, you invite; I think it's fundamentally important." Bob Craig perhaps said it best: "what's important is to be engaged with other people." What better way to do that than to begin by greeting? Then, you are in a position to ask questions.

Ask to Discover the Unknown

In my conversation with Gerry Philipsen, he emphasized the value of questions. He said, "There is probably no communicative form more valuable to you than the question. And of course, you can either go from there and say, but there are different kinds of questions and so forth, and that's a non-trivial thing. The question is the variable that makes the difference."

The use of questions is at the heart of human interaction. In his famous lectures, Harvey Sacks (1992) noted this point precisely. He said to his students,

There looks to be a rule that a person who asks a question has a right to talk again afterwards. And that rule can provide a simple way of generating enormous masses of sequences of talk: question, talk, question, talk, etc., etc. (p. 49).

The use of questions is consequential across contexts. The model of positive communication aligns with this theoretical claim in proposing that asking questions is a way of discovering the unknown. Some questions, of course, facilitate this mode of discovery more adequately.

Scholars typically distinguish forms of questions on a continuum. On the one side are questions that are "narrow in focus and restrict the other person's freedom" (see Stewart & Cash, 2011, p. 57). These questions are called closed-ended questions. On the other side of the continuum are open-ended questions. Those questions are "expansive and allow respondents considerable freedom in determining the amount and kind of information to provide" (p. 57). Across relational contexts, the dominant tendency is for people to use closed-ended questions: to control the interaction and focus on information. Unfortunately, research shows that in many contexts, being able to ask open-ended questions is critical. In medical interaction, for instance, it enables physicians to attend to both the symptoms of a disease and the patient's experience with their illness (e.g., Du Pré, 2002). In teaching, asking big, open-ended questions is a hallmark of the best teachers (see Bain, 2004). At work, Marrs (2007) showed that as people improve in their ability to interact, they increasingly ask open-ended questions. To put it simply, and to echo Philipsen's point, how a person asks a question is a variable that makes a difference in both personal and professional contexts.

Across the interviews, scholars consistently spoke about the value of asking questions and exemplified the practice in their own ways of speaking. We saw earlier in the book how many scholars asked big questions, many of which were open-ended. John Daly asked himself: "How does one question generate a positive response? Why did I say that? How could I have said it differently?" Stephen Littlejohn said: "I try to ask questions: What do I want to happen here? How can I make what needs to happen? And how can I make that moment so that it is relationship building?" Similarly, Valerie Manusov consistently asked key questions to drive her research and thinking: "Why does this [topic] matter? Why is it important?" And Em Griffin pondered: "How can I build this relationship?" These questions were personal and often used to look inward, guide their research, or the way they engaged with others.

Most often, however, the communication scholars we spoke with emphasized the value of asking questions to discover others. In my interview with Carol Thompson, she explained that she experienced an "aha" moment when she realized she could move the focus from herself to others. I could "ask them questions," she shared with excitement, "and people love to talk about themselves." Dan O'Hair explained: "I make a conscious effort to be more open to individuals...by the appropriate question." Gary Kreps said, "I realized that it was really more important to learn from the people I was consulting with." "Instead of coming in with all the answers, I try to come in with questions and I try to build collaborations." For Gerry Philipsen, a big part of communicating well is "asking other people what they think." When reflecting on this teaching, John Peters said that he will just "ask a lot of questions and have fun." "One of my strengths," he later explained, "is the ability to ask questions and get other people talking." Michael Kleine spoke of the challenge of meeting people as individuals: "You really have to work on understanding that those we communicate with are human beings. So I find myself in conversations, asking questions more than talking." Asking questions and discovering others is at the heart of how to engage well with others.

In my interview with Arvind Singhal, he said, "one of my favorite questions is a flip question. It's like one where you say, this is a great presentation, thank you, but what's not on your presentation?" Flipping your questions is an art, but it can begin with a simple move from asking closed-ended question to open-ended questions, from controlling interaction to giving it freedom. In making that move, and as many participants in this study explained, you can place yourself in a position to discover others. As you lean into a mode of discovery, you are inherently focusing on how your communication affects others. That is what the third part of the model is all about.

Compliment to Affect the Development of Self

Communication is consequential. Our communicative actions do not simply exchange meaning, but also create social reality and our relationships. In my interview with Karen Foss, she said, "There is nothing more powerful than communication. It makes our realities. You can change a reality by changing a term." With the model of positive communication, I propose that our communicative actions affect who people are in the moment and who they become. Our speech acts affect a person's sense of self. This is why the model encourages everyday communicators to compliment—to choose to support the personal growth of others.

This proposition is well grounded in theory. Theories such as Symbolic Interactionism (Mead, 1934) and Coordinated Management of Meaning (Pearce, 1989, 1994) have long suggested that people become who they are through social interaction. In everyday talk, people place the other person in a particular role or identity, a process known as altercasting (see Tracy, 2002). Through time, altercasting leads to ossification, in which people's sense of self solidifies (see Blumstein, 2001). Scholars have also suggested that our voices are blended with the voices of others. Bakhtin's concept of intertextuality, which has been extended by discourse analysts (e.g., Fairclough, 2003), proposed that our speech reflects the voices of our history. It is with this understanding that the model suggests that our talk affects others.

Complimenting is one speech act that makes a difference in developing others. When it is practiced with mindfulness, it is a choice that has positive consequences on others. For example, researchers have found that compliments made in passing, off-record, before or after a meeting helped to create team spirit and to construct good relationships (Holmes & Marra, 2004a, 2004b). In education, researchers have found that "positive statements (praise) have been found to be more beneficial than verbal criticism" in giving instructional feedback (Burnett, 2002, p. 5). Similarly, Trees, Kerssen-Griep, and Hess (2009) found that feedback that communicates respect, liking, mitigates threat is better received by students and directly affects their learning. Across contexts, scholars have shown the many positive functions complimenting serves in human interaction; it is a speech act that is memorable, meaningful, and impactful.

In our interviews, few scholars bluntly expressed the value of complimenting or described it as something they intentionally worked on. Yet, the notion appeared in the interviews in the form of an effort to affect others more positively and reflected well the movement toward gentleness that we explored in the previous chapter. John Peters, for instance, said, "being a great communicator is a question of love and of ethics…it means being kind and caring." That is exactly the impulse of the model; to move in the direction of gentleness, kindness, and love.

You may recall, for example, Carol Thompson's story about using confirming messages rather than disconfirming ones. "It was a turning point," she said, "when I realized that power of being non-evaluative." Or, again, remember how Lynn Turner explained her focus on "I messages" and her goal to offer "positive communication and try to go for the five-to-one ratio"—five positive acts for every one negative action. Similarly, Karen Foss explained, "I think I'm typically trying to make some kind of more positive move. For example, I had a faculty member come in talking about a part time instructor." She continued her story:

So this part time instructor was kind of acting as if she owned this course and so the scheduler said, "Oh boy! She is a real case, isn't she?" And I said, "Yeah, but she is really, really committed to the discipline and she is very committed with this course and that's great." So if somebody is making something in a negative way, I always try to suggest that there is another side to it as well.

Looking with a positive frame and proposing new ways of thinking is another way of affecting others positively.

Participants discussed how their impulse was to be mindful of their own communication and its impact on others. Betsy Bach expressed it succinctly as advice to students: "always remember the impact of your words on others and just be mindful of that." We need to increase the mindfulness of our messages, Tom Socha told me. "I am more open to communicative processes in the world and more attentive to them...the details of interaction matter an extraordinary amount," he added. Sandra Petronio explained that communicating well is "to be empathetic, to really, really pay attention to what is useful to people or what is hurtful to people." Bob Craig described it as a daily effort, "I need to be aware of the effect I am having on people" and "I try to be thoughtful about my communication." Kristine Muñoz explained this point well with her own realization:

> I do not like hurting people and I don't think I ever enjoyed it but I don't think I understood that I was actually doing it as often as I was. I rarely meant to, sometimes of course I had every intention. But I did not understand how, I didn't understand how rough I was being on people sometimes. And gradually I came, well I got feedback about, it is not fun for people to feel afraid, or to feel implicitly criticized, or to be hurt, or to feel not welcomed and for a long time I would say things proudly, like "I am not a poker player" or "I wear my heart on my sleeve" and it's a really good thing that I do not try to hide how I feel about people, but then I realized, "oh, but that hurts people, and that frightens them." Those are not good things. So, hiding those things actually is not too placid and it's really a much kinder way to go through life.

Being kind, of course, is another way of expressing this part of the model—our communication affects others, and we have an opportunity in every moment to be kind and gentle.

One word that participants often used to capture their effort is mindfulness. In her own research, Valerie Manusov (Knowles, Manusov, & Crowley, 2015) defined mindfulness as "an awareness of and nonjudgmental acceptance toward present moment experiences" (p. 46). With her co-authors, she explained that the mindful person "is able to focus on the present moment,

making note of any negative thought patterns she is having, while attempting to refrain from unconstructive interpretations of present-moment experience" (p. 46). Perhaps, then, teaching, researching, and reflecting about
communication, fosters mindfulness. In her research, Manusov showed that
by "improving mindfulness capabilities, individuals might benefit from positive conflict outcomes, thus increasing the likelihood of relationship success"
(p. 54). In our interview with Arvind Singhal, he expressed this direction as
flipping the script. Instead of focusing on being right, arguing, or embarrassing
others, his focus is on the quality of relationship. "It is a compass," he said,
"there is more mindfulness at every moment…because I am self-correcting.
It's more evolutionary than revolutionary," he said. There is an "increasing
focus on the quality of the relationship, which manifests in mindfulness, and
you become better at it."

It is a fact that our communication affects others. The model of positive
communication suggests that one way of intentionally cultivating high-quality
relationships is to focus on the positive—to express a person's strength rather
than their weaknesses, to compliment rather than criticize, and to be kind
rather than hurtful. This is a principle about how to be in the world of relationships. In the end, though, it is the effort to love in a small way. As John
Peters put it, "I would say the ultimate thing is love the other person. It comes
down to love."

Disclose to Deepen Relationships

Communication researchers know that disclosure is critical to human relationships. In the Model of Positive Communication, I draw on this understanding
to suggest that disclosing deepens relationships. Of course, our theories suggest a more complex picture. Social Penetration Theory (Altman & Taylor,
1973), Relational Dialectics Theory (Baxter & Montgomery, 1996, 1998),
and Communication Boundary Management each speak to the complexity of
how disclosure functions in relationships—at home and at work.

At the same time, we know that disclosure builds intimacy, often creates
trust, and serves a variety of organizational functions (e.g., a culture of trans-
parency). In personal relationships, scholars have shown that disclosure fosters connection, closeness, and cohesiveness. It also correlates with relational
satisfaction (e.g., Dindia, 2000). Disclosure has a range of positive functions;
it improves well-being, mood, and physical and mental health. In the workplace, self-disclosure helps to create trust in manager-employee relationships

(Willemyns, Gallois, & Callan, 2003). Being open and honest is a hallmark of the best leaders in times of crisis (e.g., Seeger & Ulmer, 2001). Disclosure matters in healthcare interaction (e.g., Du Pré, 2002) and is a "powerful tool in the classroom" (Cayanus, 2004, pp. 6–7). Across contexts, disclosure is a speech act that serves a wide variety of positive functions.

The model of positive communication adds an important layer. It calls individuals to engage in disclosure that is both congruent and courageous— acknowledging, of course, that this is a life-long journey. Congruent disclosure is the ability to be emotionally honest (see Satir, 1976). It reflects an "accurate matching of experience with awareness" (Rogers, 1961, p. 282) and is authentic, honest, and human. Courageous disclosure is the effort to reveal private information in spite of risks and fears. In practice, it involves (a) telling the truth, (b) overcoming fear, and (c) affirming the self. Congruent and courageous disclosure are not states of being; they are directions.

In our interviews with participants, the importance of disclosure emerged indirectly. When Betsy Bach reflected on her development, she expressed it as opening up, from not disclosing to revealing personal information appropriately. Early on, she said that she was "shy, kind of quiet" and "even afraid to offer an opinion." But today, she was much more comfortable with both herself and her ability to communicate. As she put it in the interview: "I now know how to share my thoughts, opinions, ideas in a way that isn't overbearing."

Similarly, Em Griffin described his conscious effort to be real. He said, "I try to be real, to self-disclose." He pressed on: "I want them to know who I am, partly because I like people to know who I am, but partly because it is effective." Engaging in disclosure effectively—and being willing to be vulnerable with others, was an important part of our participants' development.

Kristine Muñoz put it concisely. She said: "I have gotten more open." A little later, she echoed that statement, "I am more open and willing to express things than I used to." Jon Nussbaum aligned with the idea of congruency. He said, "I try to find ways to cut through the posturing and the face-saving." He drew on an instance with a student:

> And the other thing is to just be efficient and honest....I don't mean this in an ego-maniacal way, but I'm like the status person so I try to just say, "look, I'm paying attention to you. I realize that I'm the person here that can decide your grade or do something like that, but we can still have an open and honest conversation and I will be honest with you, and I'll tell you right off the bat, you haven't been in class. You haven't done this and this and that's a problem, and I'm concerned. Now cut the bullshit and tell me why you weren't in class. I can help."

As Jon Nussbaum described it, he is seeking congruency both from himself and the student. His message is clear: "Let's have an open and honest conversation." If both Jon and his student can communicate authentically and genuinely, the story highlights, they can make real contact and understand one another.

Valerie Manusov's comments epitomized the process I am describing here: a life-long movement toward opening up to others—to disclosing more courageously and more congruently. In the interview, Valerie shared her story with me: "I have thought of myself as a pretty open person most of the time, but I actually realized that most of my demeanor seemed very reticent. It was a huge realization," she said to me, "because it helped me to understand my own role and why some things never developed, why some friendships never developed, or why some romantic relationships never developed. I never knew," she said, "the extent to which my own fear was coming across as not being open, or as being reticent and that is not a very engaging way to be." Learning about herself in this way moved her to self-disclose more effectively. She reflected with me: "we are not fully ourselves and we can't be fully ourselves, and we can't be fully open about everything because that does not help." At the same time, "I try to get behind the mask a little more and part of that is I'm pretty able to self-disclose, not in a strategic way…but I just want to show up that way through interaction with people."

Disclosing is a way of showing up in interaction with people. Authenticity, genuineness, and being courageous in the moment can deepen relationships. As Valerie put it, "it really is hard to be open with others and to be able to engage and make contact with them." Of course, this is a life-long process. But learning to disclose more congruently can point us in the right direction.

Encourage to Give Support

Communication is not simply a way of sharing information; it is also a way of giving. Communication is a gift when we share advice, reduce emotional distress, enhance self-esteem or confidence, or show affection and love. Across disciplines, researchers have found that giving social support and affection has a range of positive impacts: it enhances the health of others, reduces stress, strengthens a person's sense of self, and provides tangible assistance (e.g., Albrecht & Adelman, 1987; Caplan & Samter, 1999). The model of positive communication, which is grounded in this vast literature, suggests that encouraging is one speech act that can be used to give support. At home or at work, the model suggests, there are moment-to-moment opportunities to support the people around us and to encourage their potentiality. Being mindful about these moments and intentionally acting when seeing an opportunity to provide support exemplifies communication excellence.

In our interviews with communication scholars, few discussed the importance of encouraging directly. It was not something they practiced every day. However, our scholars emphasized the value of being supported and the importance of being supportive. Recall, for example, my favorite story from Gerry Philipsen, in which he opens an anonymous letter and decides to build people up rather than to tear them down. Or consider Myria Allen's reflection that her focus should be "to help lift up young scholars and young students." In his interview, Art Bochner, who has been a faculty member at the University of South Florida since 1984, agreed with this principle. He said to me, "I think confidence is really, really important." He added, "I think that's one of the areas we need to work on with younger professors. Instead of beating them down and telling them all the things they have to do, that doesn't necessarily help their confidence." Art reflected on his own journey and said: it was critical for me to have "people that supported my attempts to try to do something a little bit new and different." A minute or so later, he said, "I'm very grateful to have always had people who believed in me and supported me and who loved me."

The movement to support others, particularly young scholars and students, was present throughout the interviews. Betsy Bach, for instance, said, "it's time for me to let my younger colleagues shine, you know, to help them get the recognition that they deserve." Em Griffin spoke clearly about intentionally considering the needs of others. It takes real hard work, he said, to "find out and consider what does this person need. What are their needs and desires? And if you consider that, you can adjust your communication to try and have their needs and desires met." Similarly, Gerry Philipsen explained, "sometimes, I am looking for opportunities to be helpful, and supportive, and kind, and useful." Then, he shared a specific instance with a student in which he sought to be encouraging:

> I am always writing papers and so forth. And every time, I was just saying this to a student last night, she has been having some difficulty working on her little research paper and research project, and I said: "Every time I have been working on a paper, I get to a point where I say to myself, 'you can't do this or you can't do this again' [laughter]. And then I have an identity crisis. And then there is some reason why I can't stop. I promised something or I need something for my annual report or mainly

I just want to get something done, it is something I want to accomplish here. And so at that point, I push, and push, and push, and struggle, and struggle, and go on a long walk trying to think this through and eventually I figure out some way that I've got something there to say, that I really want to say. It is not the grand notion I had when I started but it is something. And I push that through and get it done and in many instances I am quite pleased with that. For me, it's interesting that here somebody does something over 40, 50 years or so, and even when they have done this many, many, many times and it is the way they have earned their living and have some modest success with it but they still say 'I can't do it' and it never goes away" [laughter].

This moment between Gerry and his student is a gift. He is providing support, exemplifying his process of writing, so that she may understand that her experience and his experience are more similar than different. And with that spirit, he can then communicate to her that if she is willing to face her own identity crisis and to push forward in spite of her doubts and fears, that at the end of it, she will have something of value.

When communication scholars thought about encouraging others, they thought of their students or their younger selves. Karen Foss, for example, put it concisely: "Let's try to support the students in figuring out who they are, who they are going to be, and help them get there." Myria Allen gave an example of a younger faculty who joined the department. She explained how three other faculty members and herself cultivated her growth. She said, "we lifted her up. We mentored her because we wanted her to fly, to succeed." Often, this way of engaging with students was a gift they were first given by their own mentors. Kristine Muñoz received the gift from Robert Hopper and Gerry Philipsen: "I was incredibly fortunate with those two mentors," she said to me. Raymie McKerrow got it from a teacher at Southern Illinois. Lynn Turner spoke of Miss Brody, her 7th- and 8th-grade teacher. She explained:

I will never forget her as long as I live… she was very encouraging. She brought a lot of energy and channeled our energy in really good ways. If one student ever thinks of me the way I think about her, I'll be very satisfied with my career.

People affect one another. The people we meet can make a difference by the way they encourage us, strengthen us, and build us up for our future. Most communication professors we interviewed were encouraged by their own mentors and returned the favor to their own students and colleagues. They sought to make an impact by encouraging the people around them. As Raymie McKerrow shared, "what I have done better than anything else, it is having an impact on students' lives in a positive way." Steven Beebe said, "The greatest joy I get is mentoring students." The model of positive communication is a reminder that encouraging is a speech act that serves important functions in the present and in the future. And that there is an opportunity in every moment to build people up.

Listen to Transcend Difference

More than any other behavior, listening is "*the* quintessential positive inter-personal communication behavior [because] it connotes an appreciation of and an interest in the other" (Bodie, 2012, p. 109). Listening, by far, was the most cited communication behavior in our study. As we saw in Chapter 7, faculty members consistently moved in the direction of listening more deeply and saw it as a value. The model of positive communication builds on both theory and practice to suggest that listening deeply is a way of transcending perceived differences.

Research on listening shows that it matters in many contexts. Listening, for example, is critical in medical interactions in which it affects patient's health (e.g., Gysels, Richardson, & Higginson 2004; Klein, Tracy, Kitchener, & Walker, 1999; Suchman, Markakis, Beckman, & Frankel, 1997). It is key in the workplace, where it is inextricably linked to "effective individual per-formance in organizations" (Haas & Arnold, 1995) and a feature of emergent leaders (Johnson & Bechler, 1998). Listening also has "real payoff in terms of creating and sustaining high-quality relationships both within and across work organizations" (Dutton, 2003, p. 38). Listening is important in parent-ing (Duncan, Coatsworth, and Greenberg, 2009), family communication (e.g., Pluhar & Kuriloff, 2004), marital relationships (Pasupathi, Cartensen, Levenson, & Gottman, 1999), and mentoring (e.g., Johnson & Ridley, 2004). In short, listening is an important part of how to communicate well across contexts.

Our interviews with communication professionals align with the research. Most, if not all, participants called on listening as an ideal to be practiced. In fact, they highlighted the ways of thinking and doing that are characteristic of a concept larger than listening; that is, the notion of dialogue and dialogic communication. By definition, dialogic communication refers to any verbal and nonverbal messages that create the conditions for genuine dialogue to emerge. Based upon the scholarship in this area, we know that dialogue is made possible when people in interaction approach the encounter with

(a) openness, (b) unconditional positive regard, (c) empathy, and (d) genuineness. Participants in the interviews not only called on the importance of listening, but they also described the value of deep listening in light of these dialogic practices.

Without "openness to one another," Gadamer (1989) wrote, "there is no genuine human bond." Dialogue is fostered when participants approach one another with a great degree of openness. In dialogue, Cissna and Anderson (2004) explained, "persons remain thoroughly open to the particular and unique perspectives of their partners (p. 195). In the interviews, communication scholars often tied listening to openness. For example, when I asked Art Bochner what he paid attention to in interaction, he said, "listening." After a quick pause, he explained, "I think it's an openness to the other." Similarly, Arvind Singhal described the courage it takes to allow a conversation to unfold, to give it space, and to listen deeply. In this moment, he was describing his inner voice during an uncomfortable conversation: "I'm going to listen to this and I'm going to listen with an openness and in that openness I'm going to find a way to elevate at least me and hopefully you as well." In his interview, Raymie McKerrow spoke to this too: "I think the key term I probably have not used is just being open. Open to possibility, open to the possibility of changing my own mind as well as the possibility of learning [and] openness to being wrong."

In their work, Pearce and Pearce (2000) explained that the challenge of dialogic communication is to remain "in the tension between holding your own perspective (and) being profoundly open to others" (p. 162). This point was exemplified by the work of Allan Ward (see 2014), who was active in the Civil Rights Movement, meeting with people and opening difficult conversations. He said, "I found myself taking unto my own to never try to change someone's opinion, but explaining how I was persuaded of this and being able to ask them 'where did this feeling you have come from?' Even in racial situations," he explained,

> it was not trying to change someone from "stop being prejudicial," but saying "how did this come? How did you come to be this way? Because I see it this way, how do you see it?" And communication was so much more positive and beneficial.

It was approaching another with a mode of discovery that made the difference. Being fundamentally open, our interviewees told us again and again, is the heart of deep listening and making contact.

In *On Becoming a Person*, Carl Rogers (1961) proposed that we can choose to engage with another person with unconditional positive regard; we can approach another person warmly and without conditions. That is a second way of valuing others, engaging in deep listening, and creating dialogue. Across our interviews, we found communication professionals emphasizing the importance of speaking with warmth, without conditions, and by approaching each individual as a person rather than a category.

Allan Ward exemplified Carl Rogers' point. In the interview, he spoke extensively on the importance of moving away from categories. In describing his own development, he said, "my communication continued more towards the positive side when I got to the point of realizing I was always talking to an individual and not a category and that that made so much difference." I listen for the worldview of the person, he told me. Michael Kleine echoed this sentiment when he said, "I think that it sounds so simple, but it's difficult. You really have to work on understanding that those we communicate with are human beings. I want to listen," he added, "I want to respect positions that are different from mine." Finally, Tom Socha also spoke to this. He said that he hoped that at the end of a conversation, people will say, "'I feel heard, I feel like Tom gets it.'" In short, our participants imagined listening as the ability to overcome difference and to focus on the individual rather than the category they might represent.

The third feature of listening that participants valued was empathy. By definition, empathy involves "imagining the reality of the other" (Cissna & Anderson, 2004, p. 196). It is, to quote Carl Rogers (1961), "understanding *with* a person, not *about* a person" (p. 332). Our scholars reflected extensively on the importance of empathy in listening as well as the ability to take the perspective of the other. Jon Nussbaum, for example, said "you have to adapt to the person you are speaking with and you have to be empathetic and you have to listen." Carol Thompson shared: I want my listening to "trigger my real empathetic listening." Art Bochner said that when he communicates with others, he tries to "recognize how the other person is thinking" and "how they're feeling." He said, "I still think emotions and feelings is a very underappreciated aspect of communication life, of relationship life." John Peters explained that over time he has "learned how to listen and get a sense of where people are coming from and what they want to do with their life." Stephen Littlejohn communicated his own effort in a similar way: "[I] try to listen, to be aware of feelings that are coming across." At the end of our interview with Karen Tracy, my mentor and chair at the University of Colorado at Boulder, she put all of those perspectives together and encouraged us to listen with empathy:

> Try to imagine and understand how the situation looks for another person and that what you do is likely to end up being better in the long run, the more you can really put yourself in someone's—to take someone's perspective a little better.

Put simply, communication scholars exemplified that empathy is at the heart of listening.

The fourth element that promotes dialogue is genuineness and authenticity. In his work on dialogue, the philosopher Martin Buber spoke to this point extensively. He described it as moving from seeming to being. Seeming involves keeping a mask on, a façade, and pretending to act in a way that is incongruent with our character. Being, however, occurs when the individual sheds her protective barrier, is honest with her experiences, and is congruent. It is "being what one really is" (Buber, 1965, p. 66). Of course, and as we saw in previous chapters, being is a process of becoming. But the point remains that our best communication comes from being rather than seeming. And for our participants, it is a critical part of listening deeply.

One way to be authentic is to frame one's perspective as simply that—one way of thinking amid myriad possibilities. "I'm very conscious," Em Griffin told us, "of not trying to speak ex-cathedra or make it universal." He said, "I try to present something as my opinion, or an experience I had, and quite frankly I think that I'm heard better that way. I think it's more effective." Similarly, Tom Socha expressed the way he engages with others.

> I think over the years what I learned is that if I can really take care of another human being and hear them, that goes a long way to fixing problems, forming relationships, and success in the classroom. All of that is connected to being a better listener than I used to be.

Later, he explained that he is also more willing to admit mistakes and to apologize. Listening with authenticity is about being with another person. It involves, as Jon Nussbaum, described it, being honest and seeking the other's perspective while expressing one's own. For Gary Kreps, it is about coming in with questions and building collaborations by listening carefully. And as Arvind Singhal put it, it includes learning to embrace the moment—however challenging or uncomfortable the moment might be.

For communication scholars, listening deeply is essential; it epitomizes communication excellence and reflects a lifelong learning point. Listening is a behavior that is guided by the principles of openness, warmth, empathy, and authenticity. When it is done well, our participants revealed their common belief that it can transcend perceived differences and foster connection.

Conclusion

This chapter has sought to answer several questions: how do communication professionals interact in their own lives? And what communication behaviors do they truly value? In answering these questions, I showed that communication scholars practice communication in a way that is very much aligned with a normative model of positive communication that I proposed. The model suggests that the speech acts of greeting, asking, complimenting, disclosing, encouraging, and listening function positively in human interaction and can be practiced in everyday life across contexts. Our interviews support the general principles of the model, but add a layer of complexity that is worth reflecting on. For the communication scholars we interviewed, and as Michael Kleine put it, "learning to communicate is a lifelong growth process." And in that sense, the participants pointed to directions rather than fixed behaviors. Greeting was valued, but it was the process of inviting that was emphasized. Complimenting can make a difference, but it was the effort to affect others positively that mattered more. Listening is critical, but ultimately it was being open to ideas, taking the perspective of the other, and refusing to see others as categories. Generally speaking, then, communication scholars do not practice specific speech acts, they move toward a philosophy of being.

This is not incompatible with the model of positive communication. In fact, the words create, discover, affect, deepen, support, and transcend capture the general philosophy. Of course, and as John Peters explained, the ultimate virtue is love. But for most of us mere mortals, *agape* is far from reach. That is why the model focuses on small behaviors that exemplify larger virtues— for greeting, it is politeness, asking is humility, complimenting is gentleness, disclosing is courage, encouraging is generosity, and listening is compassion. When virtues are defined as speech acts, they are simply more possible to enact. But in the end, as Em Griffin put it, communicating well "just ain't that easy."

References

Albrecht, T. L., & Adelman, M. B. (1987). *Communicating social support*. Thousand Oaks, CA: Sage.

Altman, I., & Taylor, D. (1973). *Social penetration: The development of interpersonal relationships*. New York, NY: Holt, Rinehart and Winston.

Baxter, L. A., & Montgomery, B. M. (1996). *Relating: Dialogues and dialectics*. New York, NY: Guilford Press.

Baxter, L. A., & Montgomery, B. M. (1998). A guide to dialectical approaches to studying personal relationships. In B. M. Montgomery & L. A. Baxter (Eds.), *Dialectical approaches to studying personal relationships* (pp. 3–17). Mahwah, NJ: Lawrence Erlbaum.

Blumstein, P. (2001). The production of selves in personal relationships. In J. O'Brien & P. Kollock (Eds.), *The production of reality: Essays and readings on social interaction* (3rd ed.). Thousand Oaks, CA: Pine Forge Press.

Bodie, G. D. (2012). Listening as positive communication. In T. Socha & M. Pitts (Eds.), *The positive side of interpersonal communication* (pp. 109–125). New York, NY: Peter Lang.

Burnett, P. C. (2002). Teacher praise and feedback and students' perceptions of the classroom environment. *Educational psychology*, *22*(1), 5–16.

Caplan, S. E., & Samter, W. (1999). The role of facework in younger and older adults' evaluations of social support messages. *Communication Quarterly*, *47*(3), 245–264.

Cayanus, J. L. (2004). Using teacher self-disclosure as an instructional tool. *Communication Teacher*, *18*(1), 6–9.

Cissna, K. N., & Anderson, R. (2004). Public dialogue and intellectual history: Hearing multiple voices. In K. Anderson, L. A. Baxter, & K. Cissna (Eds.), *Dialogue: Theorizing difference in communication studies* (pp. 193–208). Thousand Oaks, CA: Sage.

Dindia, K. (2000). Sex differences in self-disclosure, reciprocity of self-disclosure, and self-disclosure and liking: Three meta-analyses reviewed. In S. Petronio (Ed.), *Balancing the secrets of private disclosures* (pp. 21–36). Mahwah, NJ: Lawrence Erlbaum.

Duncan, L. G., Coatsworth, J. D., & Greenberg, M. T. (2009). A model of mindful parenting: Implications for parent–child relationships and prevention research. *Clinical Child and Family Psychology Review*, *12*(3), 255–270.

Du Pré, A. (2002). Accomplishing the impossible: Talking about body and soul and mind during a medical visit. *Health Communication*, *14*(1), 1–21.

Fairclough, N. (2003). *Analyzing discourse: Textual analysis for social research*. New York, NY: Routledge.

Gadamer, H. G. (1989). *Truth and method* (J. Weinsheimer & D. G. Marshall, Trans.). New York, NY: Crossroad.

Gysels, M., Richardson, A., & Higginson, I. J. (2004). Communication training for health professionals who care for patients with cancer: A systematic review of effectiveness. *Supportive Care in Cancer*, *12*(10), 692–700.

Haas, J. W., & Arnold, C. L. (1995). An examination of the role of listening in judgments of communication competence in co-workers. *Journal of Business Communication, 32*(2), 123–139.

Harvey-Knowles, J. A, Manusov, V., & Crowley, J. P. (2015). Minding your matters: Predicting relational satisfaction, commitment, and conflict styles from trait-mindfulness. *Interpersona: An International Journal on Personal Relationships, 9*(1), 44–58. doi: 10.5964/ijpr.v9i1.168.

Holmes, J. (2000). Doing collegiality and keeping control at work: Small talk in government departments. In J. Coupland (Ed.), *Small talk* (pp. 32–61). New York, NY: Pearson Education.

Holmes, J., & Marra, M. (2004a). Relational practice in the workplace: Women's talk or gendered discourse? *Language in Society, 33*(3), 377–398.

Holmes, J., & Marra, M. (2004b). Leadership and managing conflict in meetings. *Pragmatics, 14*(4), 439–462.

Johnson, S. D., & Bechler, C. (1998). Examining the relationship between listening effectiveness and leadership emergence: Perceptions, behaviors, and recall. *Small Group Research, 29*(4), 452–471.

Johnson, W. B., & Ridley, C. R. (2004). *The elements of mentoring*. New York, NY: Palgrave Macmillan.

Klein, S., Tracy, D., Kitchener, H. C., & Walker, L. G. (1999). The effects of the participation of patients with cancer in teaching communication skills to medical undergraduates: A randomised study with follow-up after 2 years. *European Journal of Cancer, 35*(10), 1448–1456.

Makoul, G., Zick, A., & Green, M. (2007). An evidence-based perspective on greetings in medical encounters. *Archives of Internal Medicine, 167*(11), 1172–1176.

Marrs, P. C. (2007). "The enactment of fear in conversations-gone-bad at work." *Dissertation Abstracts International Section A: Humanities and Social Sciences, 68*(6–A), 2545.

Mead, G. H. (1934). *Mind, self, and society from the perspective of a social behaviorist*. Chicago, IL: University of Chicago.

Mirivel, J. C. (2014). *The art of positive communication: Theory and practice*. New York, NY: Peter Lang.

Pasupathi, M., Carstensen, L. L., Levenson, R. W., & Gottman, J. M. (1999). Responsive listening in long-married couples: A psycholinguistic perspective. *Journal of Nonverbal Behavior, 23*(2), 173–193.

Pearce, W. B. (1989). *Communication and the human condition*. Carbondale, IL: Southern Illinois University Press.

Pearce, W. B. (1994). *Interpersonal communication: Making social worlds*. New York, NY: HarperCollins.

Pearce, W. B., & Pearce, K. A. (2000). Extending the theory of the coordinated management of meaning (CMM) through a community dialogue process. *Communication Theory, 10*(4), 405–423.

Pluhar, E. I., & Kuriloff, P. (2004). What really matters in family communication about sexuality? A qualitative analysis of affect and style among African American mothers and adolescent daughters. *Sex Education, 4*(3), 303–321.

Rogers, C. (1961). *On becoming a person.* Boston, MA: Houghton Mifflin.

Sacks, H. (1992). In G. Jefferson (Ed.), *Lectures on conversation* (Vols. 1–2). Cambridge, MA: Blackwell.

Satir, V. (1976). *Making contact.* Ann Arbor, MI: University of Michigan Press.

Seeger, M. W., & Ulmer, R. R. (2001). Virtuous responses to organizational crisis: Aaron Feuerstein and Milt Colt. *Journal of Business Ethics, 31*(4), 369–376.

Singhal, A. (2013). Transforming education from the inside out. In R. Hiemstra & P. Carre (Eds.), *A feast of learning: International perspectives on adult education and change.* Charlotte, NC: Information Age.

Socha, T. J., & Beck, G. A. (2015). Positive communication and human needs: A review and proposed organizing conceptual framework. *Review of Communication, 15*(3), 173–199.

Socha, T. J., & Pitts, M. J. (Eds.). (2012). *The positive side of interpersonal communication.* New York, NY: Peter Lang.

Socha, T. J., & Pitts, M. J. (2013). *Positive communication in health and wellness.* New York, NY: Peter Lang.

Stewart, C. J., & Cash, W. B. (2011). *Interviewing: Principles and practices.* (13th edition). Dubuque, IA: McGraw-Hill.

Suchman, A. L., Markakis, K., Beckman, H. B., & Frankel, R. (1997). A model of empathic communication in the medical interview. *Jama, 277*(8), 678–682.

Tracy, K. (2002). *Everyday talk: Building and reflecting identities.* New York, NY: Guilford Press.

Trees, A. R., Kerssen-Griep, J., & Hess, J. A. (2009). Earning influence by communicating respect: Facework's contributions to effective instructional feedback. *Communication Education, 58*(3), 397–416.

Waldvogel, J. (2005). The role, status and style of workplace email: A study of two New Zealand workplaces (Unpublished doctoral dissertation). Victoria University of Wellington, New Zealand.

Ward, A. (2014). *Civil Rights brothers: The journey of Albert Porter and Allan Ward.* Little Rock, AR: H. K. Stewart Creative Services.

Willemyns, M., Gallois, C., & Callan, V. J. (2003). Trust me, I'm your boss: Trust and power in supervisor-supervisee communication. *International Journal of Human Resource Management, 14*(1), 117–127.

Young, M. A. (2004). Healthy relationships: Where's the research? *The Family Journal, 12*(2), 159–162.

· 9 ·

WHAT CAN WE LEARN FROM COMMUNICATION PROFESSORS?

My colleague Kristen McIntyre has a cartoon on her door that is pretty accurate. It's about success. On the left frame, there is an arrow that moves in a straight line from the bottom left to the top right. This is what most people think success looks like. On the right frame, however, the cartoon proposes a different perspective: "what success really looks like." The arrow begins on the bottom left, but as it moves up, it becomes a scribble of a mess, with the line tossing and turning, up and down, left and right, and upside down, creating circles of doom along the way. Then, it picks back up in a straight line until it reaches the top right corner of the page. This image is appropriate to understand the nature of success, but it can also give us insight into the process of building a career.

As I defined it in Chapter 1, members of the communication professorate are people dedicated to the study of human communication. They are individuals who throughout their careers have studied, reflected, and written on, as well as taught others, the art and science of communication. A communication professor may have many jobs: they may serve as a faculty member, a chair of a department, or dean of a college. They may be leading scholars or influential teachers. They may serve as president of a professional association or lead trainings in the community. But, at the end of the day, they spend their career promoting the discipline that gave them meaning, share with others what they have learned, and embody the nature of their discipline. In the end, they stay faithful to their profession.

This book has revealed how communication professors think, act, and grow. Drawing on 30 in-depth interviews with professors in the communication discipline, I showed that professors of communication are more similar than different in the nature of their experiences, the way they think, and why they study communication. I revealed how experienced communication faculty members approach the classroom and the nature of teaching, as well as how they grow as teachers. We saw how they developed and grew throughout their career in their ways of thinking, but also in the way they approach human interaction. In this chapter, I summarize the key findings from the study and present implications for theory and practice. At the end, I make a call to action for young and experienced scholars alike.

Key Findings

Chapter 2 focused on the nature of a communication professorate. I asked: what commonalities exist across communication scholars? What experiences bind them? And what is the nature of those experiences? Generally speaking, the chapter revealed a natural strength in communication skills, whether it was the ability to perform as a public speaker or to write with reflection. Most of our participants were shaped by childhood experiences that guided them toward this academic choice. More importantly, we found a deep characteristic across our participants: they are (appropriately) sensitive to human interaction, to what people say and do, and are personally reflective and guided by questions. Finally, the chapter showed that our participants' careers were propelled by enthusiasm and a love for the ideas, concepts, and values of the field. From my perspective, the lesson of the chapter is that we are more similar than different. Thus, the communication professoriate could capitalize on its collective strength to promote shared understanding in society.

The guiding question in Chapter 3 was: How do members of the communication professorate grow throughout their career? In answering this question, I showed the natural and gradual evolution of personal growth for our scholars. I drew on Lynn Turner's term, a "gradual awakening," to capture the lifelong process. Specifically, our communication professors grew in two dominant directions. They experienced a gradual awakening toward self-confidence and a movement toward others. As they built confidence in their ability to teach, to write, to speak, and to work with others, their gaze moved outward, in the direction of others. The chapter taught me the value of time in finding one's equilibrium. We want people to learn quickly, but it often took a lifetime for them to affirm their being.

In Chapter 4, I turned to teaching excellence. Every participant in this study mentioned their role as a teacher and the importance that students have in their lives. Early on, in fact, I decided not to ask questions about teaching, but it was impossible to separate these scholars from their role as a teacher and from the meaning they drew from students. They simply loved working with students. In the chapter, I showed how each scholar grew as a teacher. In the interviews, I noticed three movements. A first movement was toward students and their learning. Our participants cared much less about being on stage and more about whether students were actually learning. This point aligned with a second movement: they increasingly wanted to hear students' voices. They dimmed their own voice and gave space for students to do the talking. Finally, many of our participants moved toward experiential learning. They moved from lecturing to putting students to action. To use a quick analogy, they moved from being tennis players to tennis coaches: simply throwing a few balls here and there and letting students do the hitting.

The heart of the project was to understand communication professors' meta-cognitive development. That is what Chapter 5 is all about. In it, I posed the question: How do communication professors think? How did their thinking about the nature of communication change over the course of their career? What have been meta-cognitive turning points? Getting to these questions was more difficult than I originally thought. Our interviews revealed that change in thinking is slow. Specifically, the narratives marked a movement from dualism to commitment. Our participants became more comfortable with uncertainty, dealt with the multiplicity of ideas, and committed to a set of ideas and principles. The most common commitment was to view communication as a constitutive process rather than a mode of transmission. In this sense, then, our participants' thinking evolved in alignment with the discipline's paradigm shift. What mattered most was not ideas, it was people. That is a lesson I learned from writing Chapter 5: we are most influenced by the people we meet.

Chapter 6 tackled the question of what communication professors see and hear. Expertise gives professionals a distinctive sense of reality. In Chapter 6, I wanted to show how our participants experienced social reality. Not surprisingly, they saw and heard a lot of communication. They could see non-verbal behaviors in action—subtle movements of the feet, a touch, or leaning away. They also paid attention to the ways people use language. And as a result, they saw missed opportunities for human connection. At every turn of talk, people can choose to move in the direction of others, but they often withdraw. They could compliment, but instead criticize. They foster defensiveness instead of closeness. Our communication professionals saw missed opportunities in the landscape of social interaction. And fortunately, that gives us lots of space to improve communication as a practice.

Chapters 7 and 8 answered the same big question: how do communication professors communicate in their own lives? Chapter 7 focused on life-long directions. First, they moved in the direction of consciousness and became more self-aware of their strengths and shortcomings. Second, they lived with the pressure of knowing better and falling short. That pressure increased their empathy about the challenges of communicating well and helped them to be more gentle with others. Third, they moved from speaking to listening and gave more space for others' voices. Fourth, they played with language, found opportunities to be witty, and enjoyed humor in the small moments.

Chapter 8 approached the question from a different angle. Using my model of positive communication, I explored the behaviors that matter for communication professors. Although there is strong support for the model, the chapter revealed that our participants developed a philosophy of being rather than practiced certain behaviors. Greeting, asking, complimenting, disclosing, encouraging, and listening were all important, but it was the process of creating, discovering, affecting, deepening, and supporting, and transcending that was most important. Communicating well is not a state. It is a life-long process of growing and developing. As Craig (2006) wrote:

> Becoming an excellent communicator means more than just learning how to get results. It means growing as a person, appreciating the values that underlie good communication, developing the skills and character traits that naturally emerge from serious engagement in the practice of communication, and thereby contributing to the cultivation of those communication-based values, skills, and traits in society. (p. 44)

In short, effective communication is a journey of personal development.

At the same time, and looking through the major findings from the study, I am puzzled about the apparent lack of intentional practice and assessment of personal effectiveness. There is, as many scholars pointed out in the interviews, a sharp distinction between knowing and doing or thinking and acting.

Across the interviews, the participants marked that thinking about communication was the dominant frame of reference. Our participants thought about ideas, regretted choices they had made, and sometimes lost sleep over conversations they had been a part of or witnessed. Yet, their effort to communicate better was not intentional, or improved through deliberate practice. Recent research on expertise is clear that doing something for a long time does not improve that person's skills. What makes a difference is purposeful practice of specific techniques coupled with immediate feedback (see Ericsson & Pool, 2016).

If we are to make a difference as a community of scholars, we need to find ways to improve our own communication, to measure our weaknesses and strengths, to learn new techniques and practice them, and to develop assessment tools to give us feedback about our progress. We have to be intentional and deliberate in this endeavor so that we can co-create better social worlds in our own lives and inspire others to do the same. As a discipline, it means that we will need to hold ourselves accountable for our own communication and teach our students to care more about how they communicate with others than how they write or publish their research.

We also need to study people who communicate well across contexts and explore cases of unique accomplishments in the art of communication. We need to understand how a leader can transform a toxic workplace into a positive culture. We need to study individuals who have successfully bridged a cultural divide and transcended perceived human difference. We need to collect data about parents who successfully raise their children to be ethical. The point is this: the field of communication, as Craig (1989) argued, is a practical discipline. We need to find ways to cultivate the best practices at home, at work, and in society, and then do our very best to implement those first in our own lives. With this in mind, consider the formal implications of this project for theory and practice.

Implications for Theory and Practice

The findings in this book have implications for communication theory and make a contribution to an existing conversation on lifespan communication. In that domain, the focus has traditionally been on aging or the nature of intergenerational talk (e.g., Giles, Coupland, Coupland, Williams, & Nussbaum, 1992), but researchers have not examined how communication scholars themselves grow and develop throughout their lifespan, or how their expertise informs the way they communicate at home or at work. This study, then, breaks new ground on the topic that adds to literature on communication across the lifespan—study of the communication professorate themselves.

A first set of implications is related to communication theory. The findings in the book support several theories of communication. For example, we found support for Williams and Nussbaum's (2013) *Lifespan Development Perspective*. As the authors argued, "potential development extends throughout the lifespan" and "there is no ultimate end point" (p. x). When it came to the development of our scholars, especially in the way they practiced communication, we saw a constant potential for growth and improvement. Communication competency is not a state of being, but a process of development across the lifespan that involves both losses and gains. For example, we saw that scholars began by focusing on speaking well and moved toward listening. But, as one person listens more deeply, their verbal contributions also diminish. Focusing on another person gives them voice, but it also mutes one's own. It is thinking about communication competence in these terms that we can appreciate the complexities of improving throughout the lifespan.

Similarly, we found support for the *Model of Positive Communication* that I introduced in an early work. Many communication scholars echoed the principles that the model suggests and valued the communication behaviors that were proposed. However, the model of positive communication is currently too static in the way it represents communication excellence. In the future, the model needs to account for the natural fluidity that is part of the process of learning to communicate well.

From my perspective, the most valuable learning point is that we need to think of current theoretical concepts in more flexible terms. The concept of "communication competence," for example, assumes that effective communication is an ability. But the keyword for this study is the notion of "movement" across the lifespan. Our participants *moved* in the direction of confidence, mindfulness, gentleness, and playfulness. The implication is to think of communication competence not as a state of being or a set of skills, but as a lifelong point of personal development involving reflection, study, and practice.

Viewed from a lifespan perspective, we can think of communication excellence as a gradual awakening. We may want others to make the right moves "now," but this study is a reminder that one moment in time cannot define a person's competency. This understanding should be applied to teaching as well.

Often, the expectations are that teachers should learn to teach well quickly, but every teacher knows that the puzzle of teaching and learning cannot be solved. Every class has a different climate. Every student has a unique personality and character. If we can think in this way, with the notion of lifelong movement or the understanding of a gradual awakening across the lifespan, we can approach complex theoretical constructs (and people) with empathy.

This book fills an important gap in our understanding of the communication professoriate. As described in Chapter 2, researchers know quite a bit about the professional activities of professors or the intellectual trends or history in a given discipline. We know much less, however, about what it means both personally and professionally to lead the life of a professor. With the help of in-depth interviews, I have shown what the journey is like in terms of development and why it is an important one. Future research should examine the life of the communication professorate even more closely to discover the turning points, the pits of despair, or the learning points at the end of life. It would also be wonderful to know the differences and similarities across disciplines.

It is important to note that this study focused on only one kind of communication professional: the academic. Future research should examine the development and journey of other professionals in the field of communication such as advertising executives, filmmakers, public information officers, or communication specialists. We need to know more about how students of communication apply what they have learned in their career and across their lifespan and whether they embody the discipline's core values and mission. How do our undergraduate and graduate students, for example, apply communication theories and concepts throughout their lives? Or how do they develop as communication professionals? This book offers more questions than answers, but has planted a few seeds for future research to harvest.

With a focus on academics, this project has direct implications for young scholars who are developing their professional careers. Building a career is a life-long project. What the interviews have taught me is that the lack of confidence, fear, and uncertainty that is so dominant in the early years of academic life transform into a more positive energy. There is a slow and gradual awakening to confidence that makes the journey meaningful. In one of his comedy stunts, George Carlin made a joke about guys who want to be bald. He said: "you want to be bald? Do what I did. Wait a while." Applied to our context here, every scholar I spoke with had more confidence, joy, and purpose than ever. The challenges of their work did not change—but their perceptions and their engagement did. I felt inspired by that. The encouragement from the book is to look forward to the process, ride the wave, and, if you are struggling, to just "wait a while."

Second, what matters the most are the relationships we form with mentors, colleagues, and students. Every person we spoke with was influenced by a mentor or a teacher who made a difference in their lives. At work, people found meaning in the conversations they had with friends and colleagues. Looking back, most of the participants said that it was the relationships they had built with students that gave their career meaning. These findings echo the Harvard Grant Study I mentioned earlier, in which researchers studied over 200 individuals during the course of their entire lives. When asked what the learning point of the study was, the director of the study, George Vaillant (2012), said: "The only thing that really matters in life are your relationships with other people" (p. 27). The take-away here is the same: focus on building relationships, connecting with people, and supporting student success. Ultimately, happiness is relationship.

Finally, I hope that young communication professors can be encouraged to stick around in the long term. Our participants were still learning about communication, still changing their ways of thinking, and sometimes seeing their object of study in a way they could not have imagined. They could see and hear details in everyday social life that most people could not appreciate, and with the years, their voice grew more confident and more impactful. The life of a communication professional is worth it: accept the mess and stick to it.

This study also has implications for anyone who wants to communicate better. First, my interviews with communication scholars supported the model of positive communication I proposed in 2014. The model provides an easy-to-remember frame of reference for engaging in communication positively. This study affirms that the behaviors in the model should be seen as guiding principles, not a set of laws for how to act. Greeting, asking questions, complimenting others, disclosing personal information, encouraging others, and listening deeply are communicative acts that matter across contexts (see Mirivel & Fuller, in press). But these behaviors are not easy steps or a recipe for success. They are points of reflection: (a) Am I inviting interaction? (b) Am I seeking to discover others? (c) Am I building people up? (d) Do I have the courage to reveal myself when it matters? (e) Am I finding opportunities to support others? And (f) Am I able to listen deeply when my impulse is to speak loudly? Beginning to ask these questions and becoming more mindful is at the heart of communicating well.

Learning to communicate well is a slow, gradual, life-long process. This point cannot be emphasized enough. Even though most of our participants had over 25 years of professional experience in the field of communication, they still struggled to find the right words, to handle conflict, and to manage relationships. At the same time, they reported getting much better throughout their lifespan. I think anyone can learn from their general directions toward gentleness, listening, and playfulness. That's probably a good start—especially if you can train your inner voice to speak up: "let me be a little bit more gentle here," "let me listen more closely," and "let me find opportunities to see humor and play in the small moments." With that voice, interactions will naturally unfold in a more productive direction.

The findings in this book have implications for future research, for our understanding of communication excellence, and for those who are beginning a career in the field of communication or simply want to communicate more effectively. In spite of these implications, however, the study has several limitations.

Limitations

Every research project comes with limitations. This one is no different. One main limitation is the relatively small sample size of 30 professors. Although I draw on these scholars to describe the communication professoriate, there is variance both across individuals and within the group. The themes that emerged from the interviews, then, should be approached mindfully and with the understanding that not every theme will capture everyone's experience.

Second, many of the communication professors we interviewed have had a very successful career. All of our participants, for example, moved through the ranks of the professoriate successfully. Many have published well-known articles or books. Most of them have won prestigious teaching or research awards. And all of them have had long careers in academia, since one selection criteria was 25 years post their doctoral degree. And across all counts, our participants are on the peak side of academic success and in fact continue to strive. Our participants' stories and experiences, then, should be viewed in the positive side of the spectrum of professional experience. What happens to faculty members who do not earn tenure? What about communication professors who struggle to publish and never write popular books? Or what about faculty members who do not earn the rank of full professor? What are their stories? This book does not speak to those experiences, and future research should examine them so that we can appropriately balance our understanding of academic life in the field of communication.

Finally, it is worth acknowledging that the life of a communication professor is not for everyone. To be a faculty member, a person must earn a bachelor's degree, a master's degree, and a doctorate: a total of 10+ years of study after earning a high school diploma. That process alone requires perseverance over the long haul, the ability to learn deeply and to write effectively, and involves various personal and financial sacrifices. After earning a doctorate in the discipline, the next step is to secure a tenure-track position as an assistant professor, which is highly competitive. And depending on the conditions in the market or the discipline, it can be downright impossible. If a position is awarded, the faculty member has a review period of 6 years, during which they must show and document successful teaching, a consistent record of research publications, and an appropriate amount of service in their home department, college, and community. To put it mildly, the first 6 years of a professor's career are stressful and the pay, given the nature of the terminal degree, is minimal. Becoming a professor, thus, is full of challenges, obstacles, and difficulties. This book has showcased the positive side of the communication professoriate, but it is worth noting that this life is not for everyone and that many people on this journey do not make it or like it.

This study has many limitations. At the same time, it features the stories of communication professors who have succeeded in many ways and made their mark. Those stories can help us realize the wisdom of this Buddhist proverb: "It is not that the way is difficult; it is difficult, that is the way."

Conclusion

As communication professors, we have the knowledge, the techniques, and the enthusiasm to communicate well. With the shift toward the constitutive view of communication, we know that we co-create social reality through the choices we make about how to communicate. We may have different methodological approaches, theoretical leanings, or political agendas, but we can unite behind a common mission: to contribute to the creation of better social worlds. If not us, then who? If not now, then when?

In my interview with Dan O'Hair, who is dean of the College of Communication and Information at the University of Kentucky, he described an approach to interaction that he had worked on intentionally. He said, "I have always been a very fast talker and it is natural for me to be a debater. And while being a debater made me appreciate fast talking even more," he added, "what I tried to do later in my life was to slow down, to make a conscious effort of talking slower." I probed more deeply, wanting to know why. "We are communication professionals after all," he said, "we have to be setting the best examples." I believe that is our call to action—to model that communication, as Betsy Bach saw on a sign when she was young, is the beginning of understanding.

The future for my student Lacie is in front of her. A few weeks have passed since she declared a major. We are now in the middle of the spring semester, and she has been taking courses in interpersonal communication and a special topics class on communicating with difference. I go to her office to check in before seeing the dean. She can't contain herself: "I have to tell you, I love all of my courses. I feel like I found my place," she says. "Communication is so important. It is the foundation to everything." There is a power in her voice now: "We have to be sharing with people how important communication is to their lives. It is the basis to everything and most people don't know it." Lacie is a communication professional now and she is right: we have to share what we know and improve human relationships across contexts.

References

Craig, R. T. (1989). Communication as a practical discipline. In B. Dervin, L. Grossberg, B. O'Keefe, & E. Wartella (Eds.), Rethinking communication; Volume 1: Paradigm issues (pp. 97–122). Newbury Park, CA: Sage.

Craig, R. T. (2006). Communication as a practice. In G. J. Shepherd, J. St. John, & T. Striphas (Eds.), Communication as…: Perspectives on theory (pp. 38–47). Thousand Oaks, CA: Sage.

Ericsson, A., & Pool, R. (2016). Peak: Secrets from the new science of expertise. New York: Houghton Mifflin Harcourt.

Giles, H., Coupland, N., Coupland, J., Williams, A., & Nussbaum, J. (1992). Intergenerational talk and communication with older people. The International Journal of Aging & Human Development, 34, 271–297.

Mirivel, J. C., & Fuller, R. (in press). Social talk at work: Speech acts that make a difference. In B. Vine (Ed.), Routledge handbook of language in the workplace. New York, NY: Routledge.

Vaillant, G. E. (2012). *Triumphs of experience: The men of the Harvard Grant Study*. Cambridge, MA: The Belknap Press of Harvard University Press.

Williams, A., & Nussbaum, J. F. (2013). *Intergenerational communication across the life span*. New York, NY: Routledge.

APPENDIX A

SEMI-STRUCTURED INTERVIEW SCHEDULE

Introduction

Thank you for agreeing to participate in this project. I'm very much looking forward to getting to know you and learning from your experiences. My main objective today is to understand how you have grown and developed as a communication teacher and scholar. I will be asking you questions to understand how your ways of thinking have evolved over your lifetime, what communication behaviors you believe matter, as well as some of your key turning points in the way you think about and practice communication. Just for you to know, I'm very interested in understanding your *personal* growth as a professional of communication.

Getting to Know You

1. Tell me a little bit about yourself.
2. Why have you chosen to teach in the field of communication?
   a. What drew you to this field?
   b. What do you love the most about your field of study?

Your Development as a Communication Professional

1. When you first started as a teacher, how did you approach teaching communication?
2. How has your approach to teaching communication changed over the years?
3. What have been significant turning points in your understanding of communication?
4. What have been significant turning points in the way you practice communication?
5. What ideas about communication have been the most important to you?
6. How has your thinking about communication changed over the years?
7. What are some key turning points that you have experienced in your *thinking* about communication?
8. What did you think then? What do you think now?
9. What have been significant changes in your personal development as a teacher and student of communication?
10. What communication behaviors do you pay particular attention to when you communicate? What makes these behaviors particularly important?
11. What realizations have you had about how you communicate in the course of your career?
12. What changes, if any, have you made to the way you interact with others?
13. What theoretical understandings have shaped how you approach the way you communicate?
14. How has this position changed or emerged in the course of your career?
15. What do you pay attention to in your *own* communication? What have you learned along the way?
16. What phases or stages have you gone through?
    a. What stages in your thinking?
    b. What stages in your practice of communication?
    c. What do you move from and to?

Final Thoughts

1. If you had one piece of advice to give to students about how to communicate well, what would it be?
2. What else would you like to add to help me understand your process as a scholar of communication?
3. What information, if any, would you want to keep private from the interview?

Conclusion

Thank you so much for participating in this study. I really appreciate your time and learned a great deal from your experiences. If you have any questions later about the interview or the research project, please let me know. You can always contact me by phone at 501-569-8379 or by e-mail at jcmirivel@ualr.edu. Thank you again.

APPENDIX B

PARTICIPANTS

1. Myria Allen, Professor, University of Arkansas
2. Betsy Bach, Professor, University of Montana
3. Steven Beebe, Regents' and University Distinguished Professor, Texas State University
4. Arthur Bochner, Distinguished University Professor of Communication, University of South Florida
5. Robert Brady, Professor and Chair, University of Arkansas
6. Dawn Braithwaite, Willa Cather Professor and Chair, University of Nebraska-Lincoln
7. Robert Craig, Professor Emeritus, University of Colorado at Boulder
8. John Daly, Liddell Centennial Professor of Communication, University of Texas at Austin
9. Karen Foss, Regents Professor, University of New Mexico
10. Larry Frey, Professor and Associate Chair of Graduate Studies, University of Colorado at Boulder
11. Em Griffin, Professor Emeritus, Weathon College
12. Michael Kleine, Professor, University of Arkansas at Little Rock
13. Gary Kreps, University Distinguished Professor, George Mason University

14. Wendy Leeds-Hurwitz, Professor Emerita, University of Wisconsin Parkside
15. Stephen Littlejohn, Professor Emeritus, University of New Mexico
16. Valerie Manusov, Professor, University of Washington
17. Raymie McKerrow, Professor Emeritus, Ohio University
18. Kristine Muñoz (Fitch), Professor, University of Iowa
19. Jon Nussbaum, Professor, Pennsylvania State University
20. Dan O'Hair, Professor and Dean, University of Kentucky
21. John Peters, A. Craig Baird Professor, University of Iowa
22. Sandra Petronio, Professor, Indiana University—Purdue University, Indianapolis
23. Gerry Philipsen, Professor, University of Washington
24. Arvind Singhal, Samuel Shirley and Edna Holt Marston Endowed Professor of Communication, University of Texas at El Paso
25. Thomas Socha, University Professor, Old Dominion University
26. Carol Thompson, Professor, University of Arkansas at Little Rock
27. Teresa Thompson, Professor, University of Dayton
28. Karen Tracy, Professor and Chair, University of Colorado at Boulder
29. Lynn Turner, Professor and Chair, Marquette University
30. Allan Ward, Professor Emeritus, University of Arkansas at Little Rock

INDEX

A

active learning 51
adolescence 4, 5
Allen, M. 52, 53, 121, 122, 148
asking questions 29, 39, 50, 60, 84, 103, 109, 114–115, 127, 134, 138, 143
assessment 50, 134
authenticity 44, 46, 50, 120, 126, 127

B

Bach, B. 33, 41, 72, 94, 104, 117, 119, 121, 141, 147
Bain, K. 18, 30, 34, 49, 50–51, 54, 63
Baker, P. 54, 56, 57, 63, 114
Beebe, S. 19, 29, 30, 45, 47, 49, 57, 62, 95, 103, 123, 148
Birdwhistell, R. 82, 89
Bochner, A. 25, 62, 103, 121, 124–125, 147
Boyers, E. 16–17, 35

Brady, R. 148
Braithwaite, D. 26, 32, 71, 74, 146
Buber, M. 44, 47, 107, 126

C

Chambliss, D. 38–39, 46–47, 56, 63
commitment 66–67, 69–70, 73, 75, 133
communication competence 93, 95–96, 107, 129, 136
communication professorate 1, 3, 12–13, 131–132, 136–137
communication professorate, commonalities 34, 71, 132
communication professorate, childhood 12, 18, 24–28
communication discipline 2–3, 9, 15, 26
communication theory 14, 20, 35, 39, 74–75, 90, 96, 107, 129, 135, 136
complimenting 93, 115–118, 134
Comte-Sponville, A. 98–99, 107

congruent disclosure 119–120, 126
constitutive, communication as 13, 32–33,
    66, 70–73, 133
contextual relativism 66–67, 69–70
coordinated management of meaning 72,
    75, 85, 90, 115, 129
Craig, R. 18, 28, 35, 68, 70–71, 74, 97, 101,
    113, 117, 134–135, 141, 148

D

Daly, J. 20, 30, 56, 81, 96, 100, 113–114,
    147
deep learning vs surface learning 51–52, 57,
    65,
dialogue 27, 47, 57, 61, 75, 90, 103, 107,
    123–124, 126, 128–129
disciplinary thinking 4, 8, 10, 13, 18, 78, 88
disciplinary knowledge 8, 78, 88
disclosure 118–120, 127–128, 134, 138
dualism 66, 70, 73, 133

E

empathy 46, 55, 95, 124–127, 134, 137
effective teaching 18, 49–52, 57, 130
Elder, G. 6, 14
encouraging 5, 15, 42, 51, 74, 120–123,
    126–127, 134, 138
Erickson, E. 5
excellence, nature of 38–39, 46–47, 49–52,
    62, 102, 121, 127, 133, 136, 139
experiential learning 59–62, 133

F

family communication 19, 22, 25–27, 33,
    68–69, 71, 74–75, 88–89, 98, 110
Foss, K. 21, 23, 29, 31, 53, 55, 60, 63, 85,
    87–88, 99–100, 107, 115–116, 122, 148

Frey, L. 72, 74–75, 81, 84, 87, 89, 97, 103,
    148

G

Gadamer 124, 128
genuineness 44, 120, 123–124, 126
gentleness 92, 98–101, 116, 127, 136, 139
Goodwin C. 78–79, 82, 90
greeting 111–113, 127, 129, 134, 138
Griffin, E. 20, 45, 47, 52, 60, 88, 94, 103,
    114, 119, 121, 126–127, 147
group communication 21, 45, 53, 58, 60, 61,
    71–72, 74–75, 82, 84, 85, 129, 139

H

Harvard grant study 7, 14, 138, 142
human development 4–8, 14, 39–40, 43, 91,
    119, 125
hypersensitivity 21–24, 82, 84, 92

I

I-it relationship 44
I-thou relationship 44, 47
interview schedule 10, 143–144
interpersonal communication 2, 11, 21, 31,
    43, 45, 88, 102, 107, 111, 128–130, 141
intellectual development 41, 51, 65, 66–70,
    75, 128, 137

K

Kleine, M. ix, 54, 56, 57, 72–73, 103, 115,
    125, 127, 148
Kreps, G. 22, 24, 32, 42, 45, 59, 61, 73, 81,
    83–84, 115, 126, 147
Krishnamurti, J. 73, 75, 90

L

learning 7, 12, 13, 17, 29, 30, 32–33, 39–40, 49–55, 57–63, 68–70, 73–74, 78, 83, 88–93, 105, 112, 116, 120, 124, 126, 127, 130, 133–134, 136–139, 143
Leeds-Hurwitz, W. 26, 41, 82, 91, 148
life course theory 6, 8, 14
lifespan communication 3–5, 7–8, 10–11, 13, 31, 38, 43, 53, 56, 58–59, 62, 63, 73, 91, 110, 135–137, 139
lifespan development 4, 5, 7–8, 10, 43, 53, 58, 62–63, 91, 136–137
lifespan perspective 7–8, 43, 59, 136
lifelong learning 12, 29–30, 39, 52, 62–63, 70, 73, 127, 136, 137
listening 1, 11–13, 52, 59, 62, 79, 81, 92, 95, 102–107, 123–129, 134, 136, 138–139
Littlejohn, S. 59–60, 63, 85, 92, 101, 104, 114, 125, 148

M

Manusov, V. 25, 53, 56, 67, 73, 75, 83, 114, 117–118, 120, 129, 148
Maslow, A. 5–6, 14, 39
McKerrow, R. 30, 54, 55, 69, 89, 95, 106, 122, 124, 148
methodology 9, 11–12, 18, 35, 50, 57, 66, 69, 74, 128
mindfulness 13, 24, 67, 75, 92, 116–118, 129, 136
Mirivel, J. 11, 14, 110–111, 129, 138, 141, 145
model of positive communication 11, 110–111, 113, 115, 118–119, 123, 127, 134, 136, 138
multiplicity 65, 66, 69, 70, 133
Muñoz, K. 20, 23, 82, 100, 117, 119, 122, 148

N

National Communication Association 19, 25–26, 28, 33, 45
nonverbal communication 11, 78, 80–83, 90
nonviolent communication 101
Nussbaum, J. 7, 8, 14, 31, 58, 63, 81–82, 90, 95–96, 106, 119, 120, 125–126, 136, 141–142, 147

O

O'Hair, D. 22, 31, 59, 81, 84, 90, 93–94, 102, 105, 106, 115, 141, 147
openness 99, 103, 124, 127

P

Pearce, B. 72, 75, 85, 115, 124, 129
Perry, W. 65–67, 69–70, 75
Peters, J. 14, 18, 22, 34–35, 44, 47, 52, 81, 84, 112, 115–116, 118, 125, 127, 147
Petronio, S. 31, 87, 117, 128, 148
Philipsen, G. 30, 45, 52, 61, 71, 96, 105, 106, 113, 115, 121–122, 147
Piaget, J. 4, 14
playfulness 92, 104–105, 136, 139
professional vision 78–80, 89–90
progression choices 5–6
positive communication 11, 14, 24, 85, 90, 107, 110–111, 113, 115, 116, 118–119, 123, 127–130, 134, 136, 138
professional knowledge 79
public speaking 2, 19, 20, 21, 34, 43, 45, 55

Q

qualitative research 14, 35, 46, 63, 68–69, 130
quantitative research 68–69, 79, 92

questions, use of 29–34, 39, 56, 61, 67,
    72, 83–85, 87–88, 91, 94, 97, 101,
    103–104, 109, 113–116, 126

R

regression choices 5
Rogers, C. 12, 14, 18, 35, 38–42, 46–47,
    72–73, 107, 119, 125, 130

S

Satir, V. 101, 106, 107, 119, 130
scholarship, nature of 16–18, 35
scholarship of discovery 16–17
scholarship of integration 17
scholarship of teaching 17–18
scholarship of application 17
self-actualization 5, 6, 39
self-direction 39–40
Singhal, A. 27, 32, 38, 41, 53, 73, 105,
    109–112, 115, 118, 124, 126, 130,
    147
social support 120, 128, 138
Socha, T. 19, 22, 24, 26, 85, 87, 90, 103,
    107, 110, 113, 117, 125–126, 128, 130,
    148
speech act 79, 116, 119, 120, 123
supportive communication 101, 105, 121
surface learning vs. deep learning 51
Symbolic Interactionism 115

T

teacher growth (development) 51, 56–58,
    63, 122, 132, 143
teaching, excellence in 12, 16, 49–52, 62,
    83, 133, 136, 139
thematic analysis 11, 14
Thompson, T. 27, 148

Thompson, C. ix, 43, 45, 57–58, 69, 83, 86,
    102, 112, 114, 116, 125, 147
Tracy, K. 79, 90, 116, 123, 126, 129, 130, 148
transmission, communication as 70–73, 133
Turner, L. 38, 46, 55, 68, 69, 75, 94, 96,
    102–103, 116, 122, 132, 148

U

unconscious competence 93
unconscious incompetence 93

V

Vaillant, G. 7, 14, 138, 142
verbal communication 79, 83–84, 86
virtues 42, 69, 98–99, 102, 107, 127

W

Ward, A. ix, 20–21, 27–28, 30, 33, 59, 61,
    74, 80–81, 112, 119, 124–125, 130, 147

LIFESPAN
COMMUNICATION
Children, Families, and Aging

Thomas J. Socha, *General Editor*

From first words to final conversations, communication plays an integral and significant role in all aspects of human development and everyday living. The Lifespan Communication: Children, Families, and Aging series seeks to publish authored and edited scholarly volumes that focus on relational and group communication as they develop over the lifespan (infancy through later life). The series will include volumes on the communication development of children and adolescents, family communication, peer-group communication (among age cohorts), intergenerational communication, and later-life communication, as well as longitudinal studies of lifespan communication development, communication during lifespan transitions, and lifespan communication research methods. The series includes college textbooks as well as books for use in upper-level undergraduate and graduate courses.

Thomas J. Socha, Series Editor | *tsocha@odu.edu*
Mary Savigar, Acquisitions Editor | *mary.savigar@plang.com*

To order other books in this series, please contact our Customer Service Department at:

(800) 770-LANG (within the U.S.)
(212) 647-7706 (outside the U.S.)
(212) 647-7707 FAX

Or browse online by series at www.peterlang.com